Covenant
of Love

Covenant
of Love

PASTORAL REFLECTIONS ON MARRIAGE

John Cardinal O'Connor

Liguori
LIGUORI, MISSOURI

Published by Liguori Publications
Liguori, Missouri
http://www.liguori.org

Excerpts from the English translation of the *Catechism of the Catholic Church* for the United States of America, copyright 1994, United States Catholic Conference, Inc.—Libreria Editrice Vaticana. Used with permission.

The contents of this book first appeared in installments in *Catholic New York*.

Library of Congress Cataloging-in-Publication Data

O'Connor, John Joseph, 1920– .
  Covenant of love : pastoral reflections on marriage / John Cardinal O'Connor. — 1st ed.
    p. cm.
  ISBN 0-7648-0338-7
  1. Marriage—Religious aspects—Catholic Church. I. Title.
BX2250.036   1999
248.8'44—dc21   99–17746

Contents

Contents

Foreword

I am not married and never have been. There is a great deal I don't know about marriage. I have written about what I do know regarding marriage from a pastoral perspective, developed as a priest for more than half a century. I am not qualified to write a marriage manual, and certainly not the kind of do-it-yourself thing I see advertised in the Sunday newspapers.

From my youngest days as a priest I have been haunted by the likeness of priesthood to marriage, of marriage to priesthood. "How can it be, then," I have asked myself over and over during the years, "that we spend so many years in formal preparation for the priesthood, and so short a time, in most cases, in preparation for marriage?"

Is it assumed that marriage is so natural that we need little or no formal preparation? But is there no supernatural dimension to marriage? Or, if it is argued that everyone is conceived within a marriage, grows up with married parents, and learns from their example, what of those conceived out of wedlock, or who grow up with one parent, or even in a less-than-ideal two-parent family?

Always when I am personally trying to assist a couple who want to marry I remind them of how long it takes to prepare for a profession—medical, legal, or whatever—and how many sacrifices those seeking a professional degree must make. A medical intern is a good example. Even after winning the coveted prize of M.D., no doctor can continue to practice responsible medicine all his life without keeping up with developments in the profession. But is any profession as demanding as being a successful wife and mother, husband and father? My own father had to spend many years as an apprentice before becoming an accomplished goldleafer. Should we expect automatic success in marriage?

The purpose of this book, however, is not simply to emphasize the importance of appropriate preparation for marriage or to discuss the nature of such preparation. This, indeed, I will attempt to do. But I want to go deeper, most particularly by way of exploring the likeness of marriage and priesthood, together with the radical reason for marriage itself.

As I mentioned above, this is not a marriage manual. It is not intended as a set of psychological, financial, emotional, or sexual guidelines or instructions. Nor is it a text on Church law, even though one section will be devoted to specific policies and requirements. I hope that what I have to say will prove "pastorally" helpful by encouraging both the unmarried and the married to look at the spiritual, the sacramental, indeed, the supernatural dimensions of marriage as God seems to have intended marriage to be.

The Nature *of* Marriage

1

Unconditional Self-Sacrifice:
The Difference a Moment Makes

I have never known a priest who does not remember lying
flat on his face during his ordination ceremony, in a sign of
unconditionally laying down his life. Whatever has happened
since, that moment of commitment can never be forgotten.

"I, James, take you, Mary, for my lawful wife, to have and to
hold, from this day forward, for better, for worse, for richer, for
poorer, in sickness and in health, until death do us part." And in
these or similar words Mary makes the same unconditional
commitment. Each lays down his or her life for the other.
"Greater love than this no one has," says the Lord. Whatever
may happen thereafter, that moment is not to be forgotten.

There are differences, of course, in the nature and effect of
these respective commitments, in priesthood and in marriage,
but both are marked by the same striking characteristic of
self-sacrifice. Many of the tensions and pressures of life cannot be foreseen, and the unexpected can severely test the most
faithful married couple and the most dedicated priest. As long
as the parties in a marriage are willing to sacrifice themselves,
however, the marriage will perdure. The same is true of the
priest and his living of the priesthood.

Much of this book will be devoted to the similarities and
even the intimate relationship between marriage and priesthood, but little can be appreciated about either state of being

without an understanding of how crucial is the willingness to live a life of self-sacrifice.

The following excerpt from the *Catechism of the Catholic Church* provides a context for this and for much of what lies ahead in this book:

> The whole Church is a priestly people. Through Baptism all the faithful share in the priesthood of Christ. This participation is called the "common priesthood of the faithful." Based on this common priesthood and ordered to its service, there exists another participation in the mission of Christ: the ministry conferred by the sacrament of Holy Orders, where the task is to serve in the name and in the person of Christ the Head in the midst of the community [1591].

The *Catechism* goes on to show how the "ministerial" priesthood, or that of the ordained priest, differs in essence from the priesthood held in common by all the faithful. For the moment, however, we want to focus on the priesthood we all share through baptism.

Baptism, of course, is the beginning of the Christian life. And what does the word itself mean? From the Greek, it means to "plunge" or to "immerse"—to plunge or immerse ourselves into the waters, which symbolize our dying with Christ, or being buried "into His death," that we may rise with Him as "a new creature."

In other words, the Christian life itself begins in self-sacrifice. Without baptism, without the sacrifice of one's very self, the willingness to get rid of everything that separates us from living in Christ, we cannot receive any of the other sacraments, including matrimony and holy orders, or priesthood.

In the sacrament of holy orders, one who has been baptized in Christ is ordained to serve others through his priesthood, laying aside all things that could impede that service. In the sacrament of matrimony, a couple baptized in Christ are joined together to serve each other, their children and society at large, laying aside all impediments to that service.

From the moment of his ordination onward, every human act of a priest is a priestly act, imbued with the sacramental life of his priesthood. He no longer acts simply as a man, but as a priest. This, in my judgment, is critical for every priest to remember. Remembering affects his life profoundly.

No less profound, in my experience with married couples, is the impact of their remembering that every human action they perform is "different" from the same acts performed by the unmarried. Somehow, it is imbued with the grace of the sacrament. This shouldn't be surprising. Matrimony, after all, is administered, not by a priest, but by wife to husband, husband to wife. The priest is simply the official witness of the Church to the exchange of marriage vows.

Later we will speak more of the "sacramental impact" of husband and wife on each other, their children, and the world at large. In my judgment, far too little has been made of such in comparison with the emphasis on the legal, psychological, financial, sexual, and other aspects of marriage. Yet it seems hardly by chance that Jesus would have worked His first miracle at a wedding reception, or that the miracle would have been to change water into wine. How much richer a marriage that is "sacramentalized" by the living presence of Jesus, and to recognize that in the most intimate moments of their marriage a couple are transmitting His presence to each other. Cana can, indeed, be forever in the marriage that knows that presence.

2

Harmony Through the Eucharistic Christic Christ

A part from the arrival of the Pope by helicopter with 300,000 teenagers and older screaming, "John Paul II, we love you," the thrill of World Youth Day in Denver, 1994, was Dana, hands down. In the middle of the Mass, on a huge stage, this beautiful young Irish woman sang the song she had written for the day, "We are one Body, one Body in Christ, and we do not stand alone." Young people from seventy countries of the world were galvanized. They jumped to their feet, clasped hands, many with complete strangers, and sang and wept and laughed as though all had been intimate friends for years.

I have asked many since then to describe the experience. The answer is always the same: "We never felt such solidarity, anywhere, anytime." It wasn't just the lilt of the music or the syncopated rhythm. Suddenly, as never before, thousands of them *felt* the unifying power of Christ in the Eucharist. They experienced a personal encounter with Christ and encountered one another in Him. In communion with Him, they knew their communion in one another.

What so many of these young people discovered emotionally in Denver is of the very essence of our faith. The Second Vatican Council tells us: "Really sharing in the Lord in the breaking of the Eucharistic Bread, we are taken up into communion with him and with one another" [LG 3; 7; 11]. Saint Paul puts it simply: "The cup of blessing which we bless, is it not a communion in the blood of Christ? The bread which we break, it is not a communion with the body of Christ? Because there is one bread, we who are many are one body, for we all partake of the one bread" (1 Cor 10:16–17). Saint John Chrysostom puts it in his own words in the fourth century: "What in fact is the bread? The body of Christ? What do they become who receive Communion? The body of Christ" [Homily on 1 Corinthians].

It seems hardly accidental that Saint John Chrysostom wrote so beautifully about marriage *(On Marriage and Family Life)*. From my viewpoint, what he says, what those young people experienced in Denver, is the key to true communion of hearts and minds and souls, the key to reconciling differences and disagreements, soothing hurts and pains, dissolving anger, discovering and living in solidarity. Pope John Paul II calls the Eucharist "the root and foundation of the Christian community." Indeed, he says, *only* the Eucharist can create community. But what is the most fundamental community possible, the model for all other community in society, except marriage?

How does this "work"? As everything with the Eucharist, it is, of course, a profound mystery, and I can do little but share my own thoughts and meditations. The secret is found, I believe, in the reality that *we* not only receive Christ in holy Communion, but, as I see it, Christ receives *us*. Saint Augustine describes what takes place in holy Communion in bold language, indeed: "You will not change me into you as happens with bodily food; rather, you will be changed into me" *(Confessions,* VII, 10, 16).

Each of us is unique, as is every wife, every husband. Even identical twins differ, however they may look, dress, speak, or act alike. Given the uniqueness of each, even husband and wife in a fine and harmonious marriage relationship have had different life experiences, may come to an issue from differing perspectives, arrive at differing conclusions and judgments on the basis of the same data. How, then, can they achieve true, unreserved communion in each other? It seems to me that, in a sense, they cannot *achieve* it, they can only be fused into total communion by the eucharistic Christ Himself. When they receive Him in holy Communion, He receives them, melts away their differences in the fire of His love. As Christ shares in our humanity, then, they share in His divinity. But in His divinity, as Son of God, He is one with the Father and the Holy Spirit. In His divinity there can be no separateness. I would think, then, that a couple who receive and are received by Him are dissolved into one in Him. Thus an entire congregation, thousands of people, can become one, indivisible body in Christ. Does that make "sense"? It does to me, to the degree that we can translate mystery into *sense*.

Does this all happen "automatically"? If that question means, "Do we receive Christ and does He receive us in holy Communion despite our subjective dispositions, our attitudes, our sins?" Yes, we do. But as in all our relations with Christ, *we*, not He, are likely to condition the relationship. We can refuse to permit His unifying love from actualizing its full potential, from working with complete effectiveness. Christ never withdraws from us; it is we who withdraw from Him.

A couple who receive holy Communion together, but refuse to talk to each other, to look at each other, to give themselves to each other, who constantly scream at each other, or are simply indifferent to each other, or merely superficially cordial, surely prevent that fusion into one that the fire of the eucharistic Christ's love can achieve if allowed to. After all, it is not accidental that the eucharistic Christ is available only through Christ's sacrificing Himself for us. That was true on the cross, that is true, if in a different way, in the Mass. If intimate union with Christ in the Eucharist is to be achieved, we must sacrifice everything that keeps us from such: our tempers, our pride, our vanity, our impurities, even our distractions and preoccuptions when receiving holy Communion—everything we try to reserve for ourselves. Only if each party to the marriage makes such sacrifices do the barriers fall between each and Christ and between each and the other.

Am I getting too abstract, too esoteric? Is what I'm saying here out of touch with the real world of marriage? Perhaps, since I am not married. But perhaps what is taken for granted as the real world of marriage is not what marriage need be. It is difficult to believe that God created marriage for couples to be miserable, or live cold and empty lives with each other. But always I go back to the story in Genesis. The minute Adam and Eve cut themselves off from intimate union with God, Adam turned on Eve. "Why did you eat the fruit I told you not to eat?" God asked. Adam's answer is shameful: "The woman you put here gave me the fruit and I ate it." What a stout fellow he was!

Adam shattered the idyllic possibilities of marriage that God had intended; Christ restored those possibilities. In every marriage are the seeds of disharmony and dissent sowed by the sin of Adam. In the eucharistic Christ is the tremendous potential for the most wondrous and intimate harmony. Adam and Eve ate the fruit of death and their marriage was thrown into discord. The couple who eat the Body of Life, the couple who make whatever sacrifice is necessary for intimate communion with the eucharistic Christ, can find themselves in the kind of communion with each other they never dreamed of before. What Saint Augustine said of himself as an individual is surely as true for any married couple: "My heart was made for thee, O Lord, and it will not rest until it rests in thee."

3

Tempering Original Sin

Few couples factor death into their marriage plans: the death of beauty, the death of health, the death of a job, the death of security, the death of a child, the death of either spouse. Original sin helps explain a lot, like some of the misunderstandings that can cloud the finest of marriages. It helps explain excessive drinking and tensions over money. It helps explain contraceptives and abortion and jealousies and infidelities.

Why introduce such morbid reflections into a pastoral book on marriage? Realism. Marriage is lived out in the human condition, the world of time and space disordered by original sin, the destructive fruit of the first marriage, that of Adam and Eve.

The destructive force of this thing we call original sin is remarkable, and all the more so, if we are ignorant of it or dismiss it as a superstition. The first human sin ever committed is still very much with us. We come into the world critically weakened by it. Baptism makes a tremendous difference in restoring us to divine life, but we are still left with grave flaws, the destructive tendencies of concupiscence, darkness of understanding, vulnerability to illness, to death. It's crucial for a couple to realize that these are not forces controlled simply by good will, or good marriage counseling. They are tempered only by grace, the grace of prayer, the grace of the confessional, the grace of the other sacraments.

The original sin was committed in a marriage in which

both parties wanted greater power, the power to be gods themselves, to define good and evil in their own terms, to know everything about everything. Much has been written through the centuries about power, little of it flattering. Francis Bacon's comment described Adam and Eve's situation well: "It is a strange desire to seek power, and to lose liberty; or to seek power over others, and to lose power over one's self." The Roman Tacitus had said it centuries earlier: "The lust for power, for dominating others, inflames the heart more than any other passion." And Lord Acton's maxim was to become famous much later: "Power tends to corrupt; absolute power corrupts absolutely."

What was the immediate effect of this first attempt to seize power in a marriage? Both parties became instantly aware that they were naked. In other words, they had instantly lost their innocence, and the sense of freedom that goes with it. Now they were ashamed to be seen, and hid themselves. What happened next, though told poetically, perhaps, in Genesis, was frighteningly typical of what the sin of pride and the lust for power can do to any marriage.

> The LORD God called out to the man, "Where are you?" He answered, "...I was afraid and hid from you; because I was naked." "Who told you that you were naked?" God asked. "Did you eat the fruit that I told you not to eat?" The man answered, "The woman you put here with me gave me the fruit, and I ate it." The LORD God asked the woman, "Why did you do this?" She replied, "The snake tricked me into eating it" (Gn 3:9–13).

What a mess. The ideal husband immediately blames his ideal wife for his own disastrous pride. And by implication, he blames God. *You put this woman with me.* Who doesn't recognize this kind of blame-shifting in marriage, eventually ending up with, "If I hadn't married you, my life wouldn't be a wreck." The "woman" at least had the insight—and the charity—to blame it on the snake, sin personified, the diabolical tempter, rather than on either her husband or God.

Interpret Genesis literally, figuratively, symbolically, or any way you want, it confronts us with what sin did to the marriage of the two paragons of the human race, the only couple who have truly had everything this world has to offer and far more. They had exceptional freedoms that no one of us has; most importantly, freedom from death. As the *Catechism of the Catholic Church* puts it, however, "the Church has always taught that "the overwhelming misery" which oppresses us and our "inclination toward evil and death" can be understood only in relation to original sin, transmitted to all of us, "a sin which is the death of the soul."

Married couples are in no way exempt from the "miseries" and the various kinds of "deaths" inherited because of original sin. Nor are married couples exempt from committing personal sins that corrode their marriage, however wondrously it began. I make such a point of this because it is rarely mentioned even in the Catholic marriage manuals that I have seen, and it is hardly the stuff of many marriage counseling sessions conducted by even responsible—and Catholic—marriage counselors. I certainly don't recall hearing it spoken of during Pre-Cana sessions, although maybe I simply missed the right session.

Years ago, the famous psychiatrist and marriage clinician, Dr. Karl Menninger, wrote a book called *Whatever Became of Sin?* In essence, he argues that so often we turn to science, technology, psychiatry, psychology, therapy, medicines, drugs, etc., etc., etc., when our problem is sin, most destructive when least recognized. We so easily fail, especially in our culture, to recognize the cancer of sin eating away at a marriage, especially the sin of pride, of vying for power with God or with each other.

I don't expect that what I'm saying here will be very popular, but I sincerely believe it to be both realistic and potentially most helpful. "All who receive God's abundant grace and are freely put right with him will rule in life through Christ" (Rom 5:17). Every married couple can well use every human means available to help make their marriage as close to being perfect as a marriage can be, science, technology, medicine, counseling, therapy, friendly advice—everything. It's most important that they do. But Socrates reminded us of how important it is, as well, to know ourselves. It is crucial to know that as we are prone to evil because of original sin, we are prone to the most magnificent good, if we let the grace of Christ work in us. No human power of itself can rid us of the sin or sins that may be debilitating our marriage. Divine forgiveness can. That's why we have the sacrament of penance and reconciliation. Daily prayer, the rosary, the Eucharist in holy Communion, these won't of themselves cure neuroses or psychoses or cancer or unemployment or too small a paycheck for too high a mortgage. They are not magic, they are mystery. A marriage can do beautifully without magic. Without mystery, if it survives at all, it is but to limp along as a pale shadow of the hope promised on the day of the wedding.

4

For Better or for Worse: The Indissolubility of Marriage

"For better, for worse, for richer, for poorer, in sickness and in health, until death," or the equivalent words in a wedding ceremony, are at least as awesome as the oath of obedience taken in an ordination ceremony. Just possibly, however, the marriage vow may be far more difficult to live with. I'm not sure that those of us involved in helping couples prepare for marriage always approach forthrightly the commitment to "indissolubility" in marriage and what it can entail. Perhaps there would be fewer requests for a declaration of nullity if we did so.

Just the other day, for example, I visited a young woman in a hospital. She has been married but a year, has a newborn baby, and has been diagnosed with a severe type of cancer. Her life span may be very brief, indeed. She is blessed with a truly devoted husband. But how radically their lives may be changed, even if she survives. I have written before about my thirty-five-year-old nephew with a beautiful young wife and three children. Cancer has taken him. She is left with her children to face a world she never foresaw.

Prolonged physical illness, even short of death, can introduce its own form of "separation." An onslaught of critical mental or emotional illness, whether or not it results in institutionalization, can be at least equally devastating in estranging a couple from each other. Infidelity on the part of either party can be yet another blow to unity in marriage, creating a psychological "separation." The death of a child can so preoccupy either or both parties that they have little time for each other. They can become strangers, each in a different world. A suicide of a young son or daughter can drive a wedge between husband and wife. The birth of a mentally or physically "developmentally disabled" child who requires extensive care can have a similar effect. Alcohol, drugs, violence—all are capable of destroying unity. All are capable of encouraging an individual to say: "I know I promised for better, for worse, but I would never have done so if I had known this would happen. I can't stand it. I have to get out."

Am I being pessimistic? No; realistic. Honeymoons, as we commonly use the term, end, even in those cases in which couples believe theirs will never end—maybe someone else's, not theirs. Never before has there been such a love as theirs. No problem will be too great. Nothing can ever come between them. It's wonderful when a couple feel that way entering marriage, and who would want to see it otherwise? Realistically, however, we know it ignores the reality of the human condition, the weakness of human nature. It ignores the fact that things happen to us, for better, for worse, that we never planned and never anticipated. We age, we feel insecure, we worry, we face unemployment, we have bills to pay, we wonder where the flowers went.

Does any of this, do any of the possibilities cited above, with the exception of physical death, have to mean the end of love, a separation, a divorce, any kind of estrangement at all? Absolutely not, for a man and woman of true faith. All suffering is difficult. But all suffering can be united with the suffering of Christ on the cross to bring great good into the world, to help save souls, including our own. Suffering can embitter or ennoble. Suffering can demean or dignify. Suffering can corrode or purify. As melancholy a subject as it might seem if introduced into premarital discussions, or as much as a priest might feel like a Jonah for introducing it, advance understanding of suffering and its potential can be a great gift to any couple.

It is not that understanding the power of suffering makes the suffering itself less difficult; it's that it makes the suffering *meaningful*, particularly if a couple are given to the *habit* of prayer. Some of us are prone to pray only in a crisis. We don't really engage in an ongoing relationship with Christ, or with the Father or the Holy Spirit. We are not really "tuned in" to the all-loving God always available, in good times and in bad. Without such a relationship a tragedy makes no sense whatever, and is that much more difficult to bear.

I am not suggesting that either party in a marriage must be a daily mass-goer or rosary pray-er, although both habits can help mightily. I *am* speaking of a prayerful mind-set, a habit of talking things over with God, even asking Him for explanations, as Job did—talking with Him not simply when things aren't going well, but when they're going beautifully. Thanking Him. Asking His advice. Telling Him about a problem, a misunderstanding with a spouse, a worry about a child. He is our changeless friend, with the accent on both words.

I suspect that many of the couples who come to Saint Patrick's Cathedral for our annual little celebrations for those married fifty, sixty years and more, have developed their own ways of coping, as well. Their "romantic" honeymoon may indeed have ended fifty years ago or more, but their marriages have endured. Why? No suffering? No misunderstanding, no worries, no quarrels, no disappointments, no tragedies? On the contrary, one can often see suffering personified in a wheelchair, in an arthritic back, in a deeply lined face. But somehow they have used it, and are together. They wouldn't be in the cathedral for the celebration if they thought their marriages had only been for the worse.

In the long run, praying, persevering, suffering, loving far more deeply than they ever loved romantically, such couples have become so much part of each other that it is difficult to discern where one leaves off and the other begins. Might not be a bad idea for any young couple preparing for marriage to spend some time with a few half-century anniversarians. They would certainly learn a great deal that I couldn't begin to tell them, very much for the good of their marriage and especially about how to keep it together.

5

A Prayer Life Is Real Life, Not an "Extra"

I f you get tired kneeling, sit down." That was Saint Francis de Sales' understanding advice to a pregnant woman, encouraging her to use the problems of her pregnancy itself as a prayer. "Be careful to spare yourself in this pregnancy....You can only give God what you have...suffer with love what you have to suffer."

Saint Francis was only giving his pregnant woman friend the same kind of common-sense spiritual advice that he gave to everyone who asked his help, in essence: "You need prayer. Without it, your soul shrivels up. But you have to pray within the circumstances of your own life. A wife is not a nun. A husband is not a monk." Listen to him:

> When God the Creator made all things, he commanded the plants to bring forth fruit each according to its own kind; he has likewise commanded Christians, who are the living plants to his Church, to bring forth the fruits of devotion, each one in accord with its character, station, and calling.
>
> I say that devotion must be practiced in different ways by the nobleman and by the working man, by the servant and by the prince, by the widow, by the unmarried girl and by the married woman. But even this distinction is not sufficient; for the practice of devotion must

be adapted to the strength, to the occupation, and to the duties of each one in particular.

Tell me, please…whether it is proper for a bishop to want to lead a solitary life like a Carthusian; or for married people to be no more concerned than a Capuchin about increasing their income; or for a working man to spend his whole day in church like a religious; or on the other hand for a religious to be constantly exposed like a bishop to all the events and circumstances that bear on the needs of our neighbor. Is not this sort of devotion ridiculous, unorganized, and intolerable?

What has Saint Francis de Sales' *Introduction to the Devout Life* to do with a pastoral reflection on marriage?

Periodically, my associates and I meet with a wonderful group of highly experienced men and women psychiatrists, to exchange professional experiences and to learn from one another. Certain of the psychiatrists offer their services to priests encountering various problems. They tell me that the very first question they ask a priest is: "Tell me about your prayer life." It seems that some priests are surprised by the question. It's not the kind of thing they expected. Unfortunately, some of them have to admit that their prayer life is less than it should be. They get caught up in so many things in this frenetic world, useful things, important things, that bit by bit their prayer time diminishes to almost nothing, or, at least, loses its intensity.

Throughout my priesthood I have met and counseled countless numbers of troubled couples. Perhaps they are constantly bickering. Perhaps alcoholism is involved, or infidelity, or emptiness in sexual intimacies. They are inevitably surprised when I ask them before all else: "Tell me about your prayer life."

In our culture, many of them expect me to begin talking about "practical" things, or giving them a book on sexual relations or offering them some psychological guidance. In most cases, as with certain priests, they tell me they rarely, if ever, really pray, and never, ever together. When I probe this, I find that in many cases it is simply, as with priests, a matter of not seeming to have five seconds a day they can call their own. They are busy, busy, busy, in a relentlessly demanding world. Their jobs, their children, Little League, shopping, housekeeping, etcetera, keep them going to the point of exhaustion.

They are surprised when I tell them I understand all that (given obvious differences, it can describe my own life), but that prayer is not necessarily an "extra" to be packed into an already impossible day. The day itself can be the prayer. The demands, the frustrations, the rush, the annoyances, the work, even the problems they are currently experiencing in their marriage: Everything can serve as prayer.

This is what Saint Francis de Sales tells us. Everything can be sanctified, made holy. How long does it take each morning to say: "Lord, I offer to you everything that will happen to me this day"? Or, "Mary, as a wife and a mother, you know my needs. Help me, please"? Or, "Joseph, you knew tremendous responsibilities and the confusion that can go with them. Give me a hand"?

In a second or two, at any time of even the most hectic day, or every few hours, once we get the habit, we can quietly think: "Jesus, Mary, and Joseph, I give you my heart and my soul." And at the end of the day, how long does it take to say: "Lord, I am sorry for my failings and grateful for your goodness."

Can it make a difference in a marriage? I give you my word. But try it, and then give me yours.

Marriage
Preparation

6

Decision-Making in Marriage: Where *We* Fit Into God's Plan

A very attractive and talented young lady told me recently that she has been dating a fine, attentive, intelligent man, but one she could never think of marrying because he is indescribably boring. An equally attractive and talented young lady has told me she turned down a proposal for marriage because the would-be groom didn't believe in her values. Yet another, a firm Catholic, has told me she would never marry anyone but a Catholic.

I have never kept count of the number of marriages I have formally witnessed on behalf of the Church over the course of a half-century and more as a priest. Increasingly through the years, however, prior to a marriage, while helping a couple prepare, I have asked them why they are getting married. In almost every case they have expressed surprise at my question. Their reason, they believe, should be obvious to the whole world: They love each other. Always, of course, I congratulate them. It is wonderful to be in love and to want for that reason to marry. Is it basic enough?

Some people undoubtedly marry for money, some out of infatuation, some for sexual motivation, out of loneliness, pregnancy, a child to be cared for, a wide variety of quite understandable and practical reasons. Are any of these truly "basic"?

The Second Vatican Council, the Code of Canon Law, the

Catechism of the Catholic Church, and a number of papal documents all speak, and speak beautifully, of the nature and purposes of marriage. I will refer to such key sources later in this book. The particular question I ask of those who come to me, however, is highly personal, specific to *this individual* before me, *this couple* pondering marriage.

I ask why Mary believes she should marry John, rather than any other man in the world, and why John believes he should marry Mary, rather than any other woman in the world. I suggest, then, that before answering, each might ask the basic catechism question: "Why did God make me?" Then, of course, each might ask: "Do I really believe the answer? Is it the driving force of my life?"

What is the catechism answer? "God made me to know Him, to love Him, to serve Him in this life, and to be happy with Him forever in heaven."

If I truly, deeply believe this in a way that it becomes the operative principle of my life and the determination of everything I do, doesn't it follow that I should choose to marry someone who seems best suited to help me, and whom I am best suited to help, to achieve that goal? Someone most likely to help me know, love, serve God and get to heaven, someone I will help in like fashion?

Sound far too idealistic? Unrealistic? Out of the question? Not if one believes that heaven is the ultimate success and loss of heaven the ultimate failure.

But does such an approach have any practical value? Does it help a couple in the daily realities of married life? My experience with couples who have honestly tried to practice it has long since convinced me that it does, and handsomely. They have found it to be a measuring rod for every important decision and action. Where do we live? Do we try to buy or to rent? What kind of employment should either of us seek or accept? How do we plan a family? Do we wait until we can assure that each child can one day go to college? Obviously, every such question must be approached with common sense and human prudence. But it's remarkable how much it helps to introduce God into the equation. What does God will for us? Which decision will best help us come to know, love, and serve Him? Of the options available, which is most conducive to our one day reaching the goal for which we have been created? In this sense, which choice spells success?

Silly? Hardly. Admittedly it's a radically different way of looking at marriage and, indeed, at life itself. Is it simply a matter of bringing God into the picture as an afterthought? Rather, it's a matter of habitually trying to discern where we fit into God's picture, God's plan.

Does this rule out love? Moonlight and roses? Head-over-heels, walking-on-air romance? Passion? Desire? Fulfillment? Does it ignore the demands of paying the rent or financing a mortgage? Is it oblivious to walking a crying infant in the middle of the night, saving for a rainy day, caring about job security, putting kids through school? Far, far from it. Indeed, it's the demand that such realities make on a marriage that requires this habit of mind. It is these realities that demand a commitment to the will of God, a conviction that this marriage, of this woman to this man, will help each to deepen in the knowledge, the love, the service of God, the fulfillment of one's very reason for existence. What a difference such a mind-set can make before, at the beginning, in the middle, and in the end years of marriage.

At least, that's what many couples tell me after they have been at it long enough to know.

7

"Premarital Agreements" Versus "Fusion by Sacrament"

I have for some time been puzzled by premarital agreements I read about in the newspapers. These are civil agreements to "divide the spoils" in the event of a breakup in the marriage: who gets the children, the house, the car, the stocks, the bonds, etc. This is before either party has even said, "I do"!

Frankly, these agreements worry me. Church teaching is clear. Marriage is "for better, for worse, for richer, for poorer, in sickness and in health, until death." In other words, in order to contract a valid marriage, a couple must intend that it be *permanent,* or "indissoluble."

Does a premarital agreement mean, then, that a couple *necessarily* intend that their marriage not be permanent, and that it is therefore necessarily invalid? Church lawyers (canon lawyers) I have consulted tell me that in their opinion the answer is *no*; that is, a couple can sign a civil contract in advance of their marriage determining the distribution of goods in the unhappy event that they separate, as long as it is not their intention or desire to do so at the time of their wedding.

At the same time, the canon lawyers are cautious, saying such things as: "A premarital agreement could raise some questions about the initial commitment to permanence of both parties or either party at the time of marriage. While a premarriage agreement of itself would not argue to the exclusion of permanence, it may be corroborative of other evidence that the marriage was entered into with a positive act of will to exclude permanence." Or, as another puts it: "I believe that premarital agreements made according to a civil law do not necessarily indicate that a future condition has been placed upon a marriage (although such may be the case), but rather, by simply raising the possibility of divorce, such agreements betray a flawed understanding of matrimony as a bond which may be dissolved."

It's this latter possibility which most concerns me: the possibility of a seriously flawed understanding of what this beautiful sacrament is intended to be for a couple by God, its author.

The Church compares the union between couples to that between Christ and His Church, a "covenant" or compact Christ has made with His Church that He will never abandon or violate. The Church is Christ's very Body on earth, with all the unity and intimacy this involves. Dissolving a valid, sacramental marriage bond is no more thinkable than dissolving the bond between Christ and His own Body, His Church. An old, traditional introduction to the marriage ceremony puts it beautifully. In calling upon the ancient text from Genesis (2:24), the first book of the Bible, "a man...is united with his wife [or shall cleave to his wife], and they become one," the introduction says: "Henceforth, you shall be one in mind, one in heart, one in affection."

The fusion brought about by the sacrament of marriage is as the fusion of fire and iron into the white hot liquid metal that is molded into steel. As the molten metal is being poured from the furnace into the container that will shape it, it is impossible to tell where the fire leaves off and the metal begins, or vice versa. Even more intimately one are husband and wife in the sacrament of marriage, the fire of love in Christ and His sacramental grace.

But there is yet another, an even greater, dimension to a sacramental marriage. A couple are not simply fused into the one being of husband and wife; they are fused into Christ Himself. That's what the sacrament does. A sacrament not only infuses our natural lives, it assumes us into the supernatural life, the divine life of Christ, the Son of God. A sacramental marriage is a marriage exalted to a new plane of existence.

In these reflections, I have suggested a relationship between the sacrament of marriage and the sacrament of the priesthood. It seems to me that this relationship is strikingly revealed in terms of the "indissolubility" of each—each under different circumstances—always one and indivisible.

Every man ordained a priest shares in the "ordained" priesthood of Christ. The priest does not possess his own unique priesthood. There is one priest: Christ the Lord. Each priest shares in Christ's priesthood. The same Christ gives us all the sacraments, including the sacrament of marriage. A couple may marry each other civilly, but when they marry sacramentally, they marry in Christ. The priest is a priest forever, it is true, and a marriage ends with death, but the indissolubility of both priesthood and a sacramental marriage during the lifetime of a spouse, it seems to me, is rooted, in part, in the reality that Christ Himself is "indissoluble," always one and indivisible.

Obviously, there are crucial, pragmatic reasons for insisting that marriage must be permanent, such as the care of children and the stability of society, but even the pragmatic is rooted in the nature of marriage and its objective of sharing love and bringing forth children.

It has been said that peoples long ago spoke of a vein in the third finger of the left hand, a vein that led directly to the heart. The wedding band then symbolized that each one entering into marriage, encircling that finger with a band of enduring gold, was encircling the heart of the other with a bond of enduring love. Nice.

A premarital civil agreement to "divide the spoils"? It worries me very much, particularly in a culture where few people ever seem to have experienced *anything* permanent, and in which even some Catholics seem to enter marriage with the idea, "If it works, fine; if not, too bad." How many kids grow up today seeing movie and TV stars and others rich and famous who change spouses as rapidly as they change roles in a film, and *boast* about it; that is, if they aren't boasting about simply living together without having bothered to get married at all? It worries me. It worries me.

8

Wedding Ceremonies: Policies, Scandal, and "Standards"

Policies are obviously important. Without them, people hardly know what to expect or to plan for. This is as true regarding wedding ceremonies as it is about any other significant area of human activity. But to be reasonable, policies must admit of flexibility. This is one of the many reasons why pastors can never be replaced by computers. And this is why, whereas in the forthcoming pages I will spell out certain general policies and provide certain guidelines, I do so always respectful of the need for flexibility.

For example, on what days of the week or the year may wedding ceremonies take place, at what hour, where? Should the ceremony take place within a Mass? Should it be private or public? How much advance notice should be required? How young is too young? What about a Catholic who has been in a civil or invalid marriage before, and now wants to be validly married in the Church? Or what of those who have been living together without benefit of marriage? Should they be required to separate for a period of time before being permitted a Church wedding? What kind of ceremony should be permitted when they do finally marry?

I am frequently asked to "standardize" the answers to such questions for the entire archdiocese; in other words, to establish universal policies binding on all pastors and all their people, without exception. But even the Code of Canon Law, universally binding throughout the Church in the West, leaves room for local judgment in regard to various questions in applying the law. The bishop is often given wide latitude in regard to various provisions of the law. The Church is wise enough to know that local circumstances vary and, while the spirit and intention of the law must always be observed, at times the manner of application must take these circumstances into account.

I am therefore very reluctant to provide more than general guidelines on an archdiocesan basis, preferring to leave significant latitude to pastors, within the requirements of the Code of Canon Law, of course. One problem with this approach, I realize, is that some pastors can be accused of being too permissive, thus making other pastors appear to be too severe, or vice versa. A case in point, for example, is the question, cited above, of the kind of marriage ceremony to be permitted in the case of either a prior civil marriage or a marriage after either or both parties have been granted a Declaration of Nullity from a previous marriage (a procedure discussed later), or when it is publicly known that the parties have been living together or "cohabiting," and now want to marry.

In the "old days," when I was a young priest, such a marriage would invariably take place behind closed doors, with only the couple, two witnesses, and the priest. Young couples who had eloped and been civilly married by a justice of the peace would come in order to have their marriage "blessed," that is, in fact, to be validly married. That would be a private affair. So with other cases mentioned above. Our culture has changed radically. Do we simply bemoan that fact, or do we try to do what will be in the best interest of the couple and of society? I believe we must opt for the latter, and I further believe that an experienced, responsible pastor is in the best position to judge what that is, and to advise the bishop accordingly. Should the bishop disagree with the pastor's judgment, it is the bishop's right to do so, but the pastor is then free to tell a couple: "This is the decision of the bishop."

But what about scandal? If a couple have been publicly cohabiting, for instance, and are then married in a big wedding, with all the trimmings, perhaps even with the woman visibly pregnant, doesn't this make a mockery of the sacrament of matrimony? It could. It certainly could, especially if it created the impression that the Church doesn't take cohabitation seriously, or doesn't consider it sinful. In my judgment, however, we have always to ask if the good done will outweigh the evil of the scandal. I can see that's happening. I can see people recognizing the mercy and compassion of the Church, welcoming sinners back gratefully and enthusiastically. I think of our Lord's words: "There is more joy in heaven over one sinner who does penance, than over the ninety-nine just who don't need penance." (And, of course, I'm taking for granted that the pastor would have required the sacrament of penance, before proceeding.) I think, too, of our Lord's story of the Prodigal Son. The older brother became angry at the father for killing a "fatted calf" and having a big celebration for a son who had been a wastrel. But what did the father have to say? "Rejoice with me, for my son who was lost has been found."

Does it not make sense, then, that my policy is to leave to a local pastor the judgment on how best to proceed in such situations? The pastor knows that he can always consult the bishop, and inform a couple one way or the other. The bishop knows that if, in his judgment, the potential scandal would outweigh the potential good, the pastor will accept that judgment, and the bishop will assume the responsibility. This, in my view, makes for reasonable and sufficient policy, a policy that leaves largely to the pastor the judgment of what he sees as best for souls in his parish.

Of course, one of the primary responsibilities of the pastor in such a case is to discuss with the couple themselves the implications of the entire situation, to make sure they understand the moral and social dimensions and the teaching of the Church on the sanctity of a sacramental marriage. Nor should such a couple be deprived of or be exempt from a course of premarital discussions. They need and deserve this as much as any couple.

The reality is that we live in a bizarre culture, in which "standards" are set for many by television and movie personalities, talk shows, magazines, and newspapers. One recent popular magazine, for example, described some sixty marriages, of which at least fifty were second or third marriages, with some individuals having had children in a number of these marriages. The accompanying pictures showed their latest marriage ceremonies, with their children. Living together before marriage is justified by some as a way of learning whether they are compatible, although various studies show that there is little, if any, correlation between "successful" premarital cohabitation and marriage. In many cases, quite the opposite. That's hardly the point, however. The point is that the practice of extramarital sexual relations has become widespread, with the question of morality and decency often lost in the shuffle. Abstinence, virginity, and chastity are, as often as not, simply ridiculed, or dismissed as medieval superstitions, or as the hang-up of the Church.

In such a culture, the pastor has to do his best. He must teach, preach, pray, discuss, admonish, encourage, inspire. But in the final analysis, he must make a judgment regarding both these two souls, and the impact of his decision on the entire parish community. Sometimes he must make a tough call. Which is why, once again, a pastor can never be replaced by a computer.

9

Preparation for the Marriage or for the Ceremony?

If half the time the average couple spend in preparing for a marriage *ceremony* were spent in preparing for *marriage*, the whole of society could profit immensely. How can we truly believe that the stability, if not indeed the survival, of society depends on the stability of marriage and family, yet spend far more time in designing wedding gowns and wedding receptions than in premarital discussions, instructions, reading, and prayer. The imbalance is little short of disgraceful.

This is a busy world. In many cases, for a couple planning to marry it becomes a frenetic world. Life has to go on. In most cases, both parties are employed and have a variety of obligations. Time is merciless. They often find themselves breathless at best, in a state of near panic at worst. And sometimes the best of parents and the best of friends, all wanting to help, unwittingly make things worse. Everybody gets frazzled. Tempers heat up. Frustration leads to aggression. People who love one another momentarily hate one another. It's a travesty.

Every pastor can tell of couples who establish the location of a reception and the time available for a reception *first*, then tell him the date on which they want to be married and the time of the wedding. They often become angry if he tells them that either the date or the time is unavailable. They become even angrier when he tells them that they must meet certain requirements, such as procuring certain documents, responding to a questionnaire, undergoing a program of premarital preparation. For some couples, sadly, all such requirements are perceived as unreasonable, insensitive, and intrusive. They already have too much to do.

It is my privilege to be asked not infrequently to be the "marrying priest." Whenever possible, I am delighted. But I exact a stiff price, not in money—no charge, thank you, and no donations accepted—but in time. I usually ask for a six-month lead time, and for a couple to visit me for an hour or more at least every other week (every week when time can be carved out of their schedules and mine). More than one couple has decided to ask someone else to witness the ceremony. I have regretted that far less than I have regretted witnessing marriages without having spent enough time with a couple, either because they were too busy or I was, and we settled for their doing a "pre-Cana" weekend or something of the sort. The truth is that, with respect and gratitude for "pre-Cana" activities, I flat-out disagree with the common practice of a few "pre-Cana" Sundays or a weekend as the sole preparation. How can we even pretend to be serious about marriage if that's the extent of the preparation? I recognize how strapped our priests are. Further, I am well aware that I, personally, have the luxury of rarely accepting the wedding of more than a couple or two at a time, in my present job. (It wasn't always thus. I would work with many couples, and demand the same of each.)

I sincerely believe, however, that there are many ways of providing sound premarital preparation at the parish level without requiring excessive additional effort on the part of the priest. Many married couples can help a great deal. A number of married deacons can be especially helpful. Some fine videotapes on marriage are now available. A diocesan family life office can provide some excellent instructional materials. If the priest can have a session at the beginning and a session at the end of a series of meetings conducted by other competent and experienced individuals or responsible married couples, a great deal can be accomplished. This is particularly true when the couple are given some solid reading material that someone then reviews with them.

I am, of course, deeply grateful to those who conduct our "pre-Cana" and other premarital sessions. I don't know what we would do without them. But they are simply not enough—not nearly enough. Not when both the happiness of a marriage, the good of prospective children, and the future of society itself are at stake—to say nothing of the health of the Church.

We must face the reality, however guilty it makes us feel as a Church. The reality is that we far too frequently pay lip service to premarital preparation, yet wring our hands over every divorce. I blame no one, except, perhaps, myself as bishop, for demanding too many things of our priests and providing them too little help. Wherever the fault is, however, we had better fix it, and fix it very soon. Unless I am mistaken, we now have in our country the highest divorce rate of any country in history. Nor is divorce the only problem. We have far and away too many marriages that never live up to their potential because couples have never learned or even thought about what their potential might be.

I started this section of my reflection on marriage, however, by expressing concern over the inordinate amount of time and energy put in on the "trimmings" surrounding marriage, at the expense of the spiritual and mental preparation critically needed. So often I have known young couples who wanted to put their time and energy into preparing mentally and spiritually for marriage, hoping for a Mass, a small gathering of relatives and friends, the expenditure of a modest amount of money, at most, and minimal demands, financial or otherwise, on members of their wedding party. Before they know it, their plans become the victims of a "friendly takeover," and their worst fantasies are realized.

This is no small matter. Indeed, not infrequently, lasting enmities are formed, between the bride's and the groom's family, between the invited and the uninvited, between bridesmaids and would-be bridesmaids, ushers and would-be ushers. Is any of it born out of malice? Rarely. It *is*, however, far too often the result of emphasizing the marriage *ceremony*, which, with even the most elaborate "trimmings"—receptions, etc.— is fleeting, at the expense of the *marriage* itself, which is intended to be until death.

Does all this sound like a fussy celibate who doesn't understand or appreciate the wonders of a wedding day and the joy deserved by all? I'm sorry if it does, not because I mind being criticized, but because I mind what's happening to marriage.

Marital
Relations

10

A Channel of Grace to Each Other

In the zoo's-eye view of marriage routinely depicted in the movies and TV, nothing would be lampooned faster than the story told me by a couple whose marriage had become empty. Once deeply in love, now much that had fulfilled them left them cold and uninterested. They turned finally to a counselor recommended by a wise priest friend.

As with so many couples, they wanted before all else to discuss with the counselor their unsatisfactory "sex life." He listened sympathetically, but for only a brief period of time before asking them to put that issue on hold and tell him what they thought about money. Annoyed but cooperative, they began reflecting on the subject, surprised to discover the reflection required several sessions, and that it seemed to lead somehow into a discussion of their drinking habits. Other discussions of other issues followed.

A number of sessions passed with no reference to their "sex life" before the counselor asked them to speak of their prayer life and its relationship to their marriage. The question seemed inappropriate, too intimate, too intrusive and, most of all, unrelated to what they saw as their problem. Actually, they did pray, each of them individually, and were faithful Mass attendees. However, neither the prayers nor the Masses seemed to help.

The counselor asked them to think about doing something he knew they would consider absurd, if not outrageous, but first he reminded them that theirs was a sacramental marriage. They had married in the presence of a priest and two witnesses, with no impediments to their marriage. They had exchanged vows. They had ministered the sacrament to each other. What did they think that meant? What did it mean to their marriage at this moment? Schooled reasonably in their faith, able to define a sacrament, they yet had to admit they had never thought of it in practical terms, except that it meant they couldn't get divorced and remarried because they had been married in the Church.

The counselor proposed what I spoke of earlier in these pages, of how each party becomes a channel of grace to the other, how divine life flows through each into the marriage by way of the sacrament. This did not occur simply on their wedding day, as they exchanged vows. It continues throughout all the days of their married life in all that they do, including the exercise of their marriage relations, the consummation of their marriage. He asked if they had ever thought about the fact that this intimate union, however passionate or pleasurable it might be, can be a channel of grace in a sacramental marriage? "One in mind, one in heart, one in affections," a couple are engaging in a potentially sacred action. Physical and sexual, it can be simultaneously a profoundly spiritual experience. Open to the transmission of human life, it can be an instrument of divine life, as well.

If this be so, would the couple in counseling be willing to pray a prayer *together* and light a votive candle when about to engage in marriage relations? That was the "preposterous" question the counselor asked. They were astonished. Who would ever dream of doing such a thing? Was he completely naive about sexual matters? Is this why he had avoided talking about their problem?

No, he was not naive. He was a happily married man with four children. Yes, someone would dream of doing such a thing. In fact, it was what he and his wife considered to be a key to their own fulfillment. Indeed, he had not been avoiding their problem; he had been helping them to discover the context of their problem. He had been leading them far deeper into their marriage than into their problem, which was hardly more than a symptom.

To make a long story short, it would be inadequate to say that the couple have recovered the satisfaction they had lost. They have gone far beyond recovery to discovery. They are still probing the depths of the inexhaustible mystery of their sacramental marriage. They steadily replenish their supply of votive candles.

I have counseled too many couples through the years to believe I know a fraction of what they know by experience concerning certain aspects of marriage. But I do listen carefully, and when I hear a true story that has helped a couple such as the one I recounted above, I gladly pass it on. That I have done many times. Not every couple has followed suit. Many have, and their marriages have lived to tell the tale.

Every couple is unique, of course. It would be a foolish or even dangerous marriage counselor who pretended that any single solution fits every problem. I am convinced, however, that no couple can lose by probing the sacramentality of their marriage far more deeply than most people do. Hence, I never hesitate, inappropriate or even sacrilegious as it might appear to some, I never hesitate to compare lighting a candle during the sacred intimacies of marriage to lighting candles during the holy sacrifice of the Mass. Each expresses awareness of the presence of the Sacred One.

Hardly the stuff of a TV sitcom.

11

Marital Relations
and Consecration

When I, as a priest, say over a piece of bread, "This is my Body," I believe passionately that the bread actually becomes the body of Christ. When I say over a chalice of wine, "This is my Blood," I believe with equal passion that the wine truly becomes the blood of Christ. If I did not believe this with all my being, I don't know what else I *could* believe. Indeed, as Pope John Paul II reminds us, the Eucharist is the very reason for the ordained priesthood.

At the same time, I know as a priest that I am simply the instrument through which the Holy Spirit of God breathes life into the bread, into the wine, transforming the one into the body, the other into the blood, of Christ. The Son of God is "conceived" and "born" onto the altar by the same power that conceived Him in the womb of Mary, who laid Him in a manger in Bethlehem.

Earlier I spoke of the striking similarities between the priesthood and marriage. Shocking as it may seem to some, from my viewpoint such a similarity is revealed in a special way in terms of the intimacies we call marital relations and the consecration of the Mass. As the priest offers the elements of bread and wine in the Mass, the couple offer the two elements of their own bodies. The bread is powerless in itself, as is the wine. Only the breath of God can bring forth from such

43

His own Son. Each of the two elements of the bodies of the man and the woman is powerless in itself to conceive a child. Only the breath of God can make this possible. In this sense, every child is as much a child of God as was Jesus, infant of Bethlehem.

Both marital relations and the offering of the priest at the altar, then, can be seen as acts of "consecration," each deserving of its own form of reverence. And as the Eucharist is the priest's primary reason for being—to serve as an instrument for the "conception" of the Son of God on the altar—so the primary reason for marital relations, together with the expression and consummation of love, is to serve as an instrument for conceiving children of God.

I speak analogously, of course. The Eucharist is the Eucharist. Marriage is marriage. But the twain do meet, it seems to me, in ways mysteriously and infinitely beyond my ability to fathom, much less express. I suspect, however, that I am not alone in sensing the mysterious intertwining of marriage and the altar of the Eucharist. Witness the letter I received while I first wrote the above. I conceal identities out of respect for the privacy of all involved; otherwise the letter is printed here verbatim.

Dear Cardinal O'Connor,

I've been reading your Pastoral on Marriage in *Catholic New York* and being a twenty-eight-year veteran of better, worse, richer, poorer, sickness and health, I appreciate your words of support.

My daughter became engaged last weekend and I thought you would enjoy hearing how her delightful young man "popped the question." Around nine o'clock

Saturday evening he told her he wanted to go to church and say a prayer. Aided and abetted by our pastor he brought her to the beautiful new church which you recently consecrated, and after kneeling and saying some prayers he took her hand and led her to a chair in front of the altar. On his knees, in the presence of God and all the saints, he proposed and gave her a beautiful ring. I hope they're always as happy as they were that night, but if sorrow or trials befall them I'm sure Christ and His Blessed Mother will give them the strength to survive anything.

Their intelligence, attractiveness, and personalities all but assure their success in this world but they haven't lost sight of, or forgotten to thank, the Bestower of those blessings. If they are the future of the Church, I think we'll be in good shape for the next millennium.

Our pastor blessed them and the ring that evening, and two other priests gave their blessings Sunday after Mass. Would you add a prayer that their love and faith will increase and grow stronger each day for the rest of their lives?

I offer this reflection to the couple named. And it is only that: a spiritual reflection, with no pretense of being a profound theological discourse or a formal presentation of Church teaching. Indeed, while others more learned may disagree with my reflection or even consider it theologically unthinkable, I have found it pastorally helpful to a number of couples. If nothing else, it helps my own priesthood a great deal and reveals to me as I offer the holy sacrifice of the Mass how very intimate the love of Jesus is. Should it surprise us, really, to find both the most intimate expression of human love and the most eloquent expression of divine love in the sacrifice of the One who is both human and divine?

Or should it seem strange that the more I meditate on my priesthood, the closer I feel to you who are married, you who will marry in the Lord? We need not envy one another. There is love in abundance in both our ways of life.

12

Birth Control? True Love Desires to Reproduce Itself

A sure way to be accused of burying my head in the sand is to suggest that hostility toward Church teaching on "birth control" is not nearly so universal among Catholics as some reports would have us believe. I find that for a number of Catholics it is a troublesome teaching; a number of others respect it, but believe it impossible for them to practice; still others, many others, simply don't understand it. That some consider it absurd, of course, cannot responsibly be denied.

Should it be surprising that there is so much confusion about this teaching? Where are young people to learn of it? How much time is honestly spent on it in our schools, our catechetical programs, our preaching? How many parents address the matter seriously and sincerely with their sons and daughters? Indeed, what example do young people receive from their parents in this regard? How many marriage-preparation programs spend any real time on the issue? Does every priest feel comfortable in speaking about it in helping couples prepare for marriage, or even in the confessional?

I ask none of these questions in a spirit of criticism. I know the prevailing mood and believe I understand it. But if the teaching is not spelled out in such circumstances as mentioned above, how are people to know it, or to believe the Church really means it?

Weigh such silence in teaching against the powers in opposition. "Safe sex" has virtually become a national slogan, extended far beyond the question of infectious disease. Much television makes a mockery of abstinence. Newspaper editorials ridicule Church teaching in opposition to the use of condoms. Huge, wealthy foundations spend fortunes in trying to spread contraception throughout the world. National and international organizations and even conferences sponsored by the United Nations drum the same theme. Pundits argue, with what superficially sounds so wise and so noble, that if the Church really wanted to reduce the number of abortions, she would support the use of contraceptives. (They ignore the reality that the numbers of abortions have risen as contraceptives have become widespread.)

I am not speaking now of the very real problems confronted by some couples in their marriages: illness, real danger in a pregnancy, financial difficulties, poor housing, inability to care for an additional child, and other problems. Some situations can be heartbreaking. More on these later.

Nor do I speak at this moment of couples who simply believe it is impossible for them to observe Church teaching in this matter. The temptations seem to them too powerful, the circumstances of their lives, such as periodic separations and brief reunions, and other forces seem beyond their ability to control. More later on these, as well.

I am speaking largely of ignorance of Church teaching and the pressure of forces opposed to Church teaching. What follows, then, is the formal teaching of the Church as presented verbatim in the new *Catechism of the Catholic Church*. Formal teaching is usually presented in formal language, as in the *Catechism*. Later, we can reflect on it in a less formal way.

Fruitfulness is a gift, an *end of marriage*, for conjugal love naturally tends to be fruitful. A child does not come from outside as something added on to the mutual love of the spouses, but springs from the very heart of that mutual giving, as its fruit and fulfillment. So the Church, which "is on the side of life" teaches that "each and every marriage act must remain open to the transmission of life." "This particular doctrine, expounded on numerous occasions by the Magisterium, is based on the inseparable connection, established by God, which man on his own initiative may not break, between the unitive significance and the procreative significance which are both inherent to the marriage act" [2366].

Called to give life, spouses share in the creative power and fatherhood of God. "Married couples should regard it as their proper mission to transmit human life and to educate their children; they should realize that they are thereby *cooperating with* the love of *God the Creator* and are, in a certain sense, its interpreters. They will fulfill this duty with a sense of human and Christian responsibility" [2367].

A particular aspect of this responsibility concerns the *regulation of births.* For just reasons, spouses may wish to space the births of their children. It is their duty to make certain that their desire is not motivated by selfishness but is in conformity with the generosity appropriate to responsible parenthood. Moreover, they should conform their behavior to the objective criteria of morality... [2368].

"By safeguarding both these essential aspects, the unitive and the procreative, the conjugal act preserves in its fullness the sense of true mutual love and its orientation toward man's exalted vocation to parenthood" [2369].

Periodic continence, that is, the methods of birth regulation based on self-observation and the use of infertile periods, is in conformity with the objective criteria of morality. These methods respect the bodies of the spouses, encourage tenderness between them, and favor the education of an authentic freedom. In contrast, "every action which, whether in anticipation of the conjugal act, or in its accomplishment, or in the development of its natural consequences, proposes, whether as an end or as a means, to render procreation impossible" is intrinsically evil... [2370].

"Let all be convinced that human life and the duty of transmitting it are not limited by the horizons of this life only: their true evaluation and full significance can be understood only in reference to *man's eternal destiny*" [2371].

All of which seems to me a reminder that all true love strongly desires to reproduce itself.

13

The "Love/Life Link" Willed by God

My father taught me many of the most important things I ever learned. One was that if someone could do something better than you, don't pretend otherwise. Encourage him or her to do it.

Monsignor William B. Smith, Ph.D., professor of Moral Theology can "do" the Church's moral teaching on *Humanae Vitae*, Pope Paul VI's encyclical on human life, far better than I. So I asked him, as one of the best moral theologians in the country in my judgment, to do this chapter on contraception, not in technical, but in straightforward language. Here's what he has written, word for word.

Regarding Contraception

Marriage is, by God's design, a covenant of love and life. This is the teaching of the Council (1965), of the *Catechism* (1992), and preeminently the teaching of Pope John Paul II (*Familiaris Consortio* [1981] and his "Letter To Families" [1994]).

Very much at the moral core of this covenant of love and life that we call marriage is the encyclical teaching of *Humanae Vitae* (1968): "the inseparable connection, willed by God...between the *unitive* and *procreative* meaning inherent in the conjugal act" (HV, n. 12).

Frequently, Pope John Paul II has asked Christian writers and thinkers to illustrate more clearly "the biblical foundations, ethical grounds, and personalist reasons" behind this teaching. Biblical foundations need not mean so-called proof texts; but rather true foundations—principles and teachings clearly taught in holy Scripture that support the same inseparable link between love and life. The truth about love and life.

The divine design for love and life in marriage begins in the first book of the Bible, Genesis. First, love, *unitive* love: "For this reason a man leaves his father and mother, cleaves to his wife and the two become one flesh" (Gn 2:24). The Lord Jesus repeats the same truth about unitive love: "for this reason a man shall leave his father and mother and the two shall become as one. They are no longer two but one flesh" (Mk 10:7–8), as does Saint Paul (Eph 5:31).

Next, life, *procreative* life. Again, the book of Genesis addresses our first parents: "to increase and multiply" (Gn 1:28). The whole Bible teaches that life is a blessing, not a curse; it is the original blessing. Indeed, "apart from Him nothing came to be" (Jn 1:3).

Just as, in the beginning, all life comes out of God's generous decision not to be self-enclosed, so too in marriage, the covenant of love and life, all real life is connected to real love and all real love is connected with real life. It is God's own design for love and life, ours too.

This love-life link, this inseparable connection willed by God, is always at risk in any complete use of human sexuality and is always violated in artificial contraception. Scripture teaches that we must not separate what God has joined together. Thus God's design for love and life in marriage is His plan to which we are administrators, not arbiters; of which we are ministers, not manipulators.

The Church does not teach that married couples should have as many children as physically possible, but only those children they can responsibly provide for. But to fulfill or to postpone the actualization of this blessing, only moral means—only means that truly respect the good of love and the good of life—are acceptable. Thus the artificial manufacture of human life apart from unitive love is just as much a distortion of the divine design as the artificial prevention of human life within unitive love. The teaching is not that God's design be realized in every instance, but not to act against God's design in any instance.

No one of us on earth is self-created; not one! We are all the fruit of love—a generous parental love that is neither self-contained nor self-enclosed. This is Gospel love—a love that gives and serves. A great danger today is not this or that misuse of human sexuality, but the greater danger that human sexuality is truly meaningless—really meaningless awaiting only my designer use: now for procreation, now for recreation, whatever design I choose to impose on it.

A wise twentieth-century papal voice invites us all not to reduce sexuality to some personal invention nor expand it as a therapeutic fix for every problem; rather, he asks us to think and to pray over the biblical foundations, ethical grounds, and personalist reasons found in the wise designs of our Creator and Savior.

Well put, Monsignor Smith. Crisp and clear as always. You never fail to teach me a lesson.

14

Church Teaching
on Contraception

In the early nineties Dr. Janet Smith wrote of a student group at a major Catholic university that wanted a speaker who would explain what the Church teaches on contraception. She says they found to their astonishment that not one professor in a theology department of over thirty "was willing to give a public lecture explaining and defending the Church's teaching on contraception." That teaching had, of course, been spelled out in detail in 1968 by Pope Paul VI in his famous encyclical on human life, *Humanae Vitae*. Indeed, writing on the same encyclical back in 1988, in the journal *Thirty Days*, one Lucio Brunelli called his article, "The Pill That Divided the Church."

In my judgment, there are substantial numbers of couples who erroneously but understandably believe they are doing the responsible thing by using some sort of artificial contraceptive device to prevent children they believe they can't afford, can't take care of, cannot conceive safely, and so forth. Many of them have not only never heard Church teaching clearly spelled out, with all its very sound reasons, they have heard the teaching rejected or even ridiculed by teachers or others in "authoritative" positions.

We are told in the Acts of the Apostles of the high-ranking Ethiopian official reading the prophet Isaiah, who was asked by the apostle Philip, "Do you understand what you are reading?" The official replied, "How can I understand, unless someone explains it to me?" Philip gave him a good explanation. The Ethiopian asked to be baptized on the spot.

I fear that too many of us charged with the responsibility to do so have not taught what the Church teaches about contraception, or haven't taught it clearly, or haven't taught it seriously, or haven't taught it as if we believe it ourselves.

And now, as of this writing, the Congress of the United States has seen fit to authorize every federal health clinic in the country to give condoms and birth-control pills to children as young as thirteen, without the consent or even notification of their parents.

The *Catechism of the Catholic Church* is, if anything, even clearer and stronger in spelling out the Church's teaching on contraception than is *Humanae Vitae* itself. That teaching has been even more profoundly explored and clearly explained by the writings of Pope John Paul II. I have tried to present these teachings as clearly as I can, with the help of others. Pope John Paul II has urged theologians to illuminate more clearly "the biblical foundations, the ethical grounds and the personalistic reasons" behind *Humanae Vitae*. This I tried to do, but admittedly in little more than outline form. The issues deserve extensive reading, thought, discussion, prayer.

As complete a reader as I know for any couple willing to give serious attention to the encyclical is Dr. Janet Smith's *Why Humanae Vitae Was Right*. This is a collection of essays by theologians and others. It is not light reading, but marriage and its purposes are not passing fancies. Another excellent, concise explanation is Dr. Janet Smith's audiotape, *Contraception: Why Not?* What Chesterton said about Christianity can frequently be said of Church teaching on contraception: It is not that it has been tried and found wanting, it is that it has been found difficult and not tried.

Other Common Challenges to Married Love

15

Money: Source of Evil?

*For the love of money is a source of all kinds of evil. Some
have been so eager to have it that they have wandered away
from the faith and have broken their hearts with many sorrows* (1 Tim 6:10).

This warning from the Letter to Timothy, written some
time during the first century, is one of the most critical
bits of advice I pass on to every couple I help prepare for
marriage and to every couple experiencing problems in marriage, whatever such problems may *seem* to be. And rarely,
very rarely, do they believe me. I still make a point of it, hoping that at least if a money problem does rear its ugly head,
even disguised as something else, they'll recognize it for what
it is, and not try to solve what it isn't.

Notice that the Letter to Timothy speaks not of the posses-
sion of money, but of the *love* of money. My experience with
couples is that money can symbolize power, privacy, dependency or independency, control or other forces hostile to unity,
harmony, and intimacy in marriage. The "his and her" or the
"mine and yours" division of money and goods, rather than
making for good order and understanding, can breed all sorts
of resentments. Why?

First, the entire notion of two unique individuals, *this* man,
this woman, trying to become fused into one being, one in
mind, one in heart, one in body, one in affections, is exceed-

ingly demanding even when each turns *everything* over, including their individual beings, into the new and unique being we call marriage. It becomes far harder when *anything* is held back—spiritual, mental, moral, emotional, physical, or material. Instantly, in the mind of either party or the minds of both, a condition has been placed on the unconditional. "I give you 95 percent of myself."

Second, a single person normally is free to dispose of income at will: pay the rent or not, buy a car or not, give free drinks to the house or not, etc. That's a freedom that must be freely surrendered, that is, subordinated to the marriage unit, in which one no longer has exclusive right even to one's own body. Some single-life habits can be hard to break. Yet in marriage, significant decisions must be bilateral: to buy a home or to rent, to trade in an old car or keep it, to buy insurance, to have babies, to select schools for children, to do *anything* really important. But who determines what is important? Ah, there's the rub. That's when the fur can fly and the name-calling begin: stingy, miser, spendthrift, selfish, etc.

Three is a corollary of two. Who is the primary breadwinner? Is each a breadwinner? Does each, then, control what he or she earns? "I earn the money. I'll determine how it's to be spent." Where's the unity of marriage? Does the primary breadwinner force a sense of dependency on the other party or on the children? Does a wife, particularly, have to accept physical or emotional abuse, infidelity or drunkenness, because financially dependent on a husband? How many couples have I met who think they have a "sexual" problem, when the real problem is either an overt, continuing battle over money or hidden resentment expressed "sexually."

Four is similar. "He can't buy the kids new shoes, but he

never fails to have liquor in the house." Or, "I can't trust her with money, she's a gambling addict." How often we hear the argument, "We can't afford children; all our money goes into a mortgage." Or, "We can't have a second child; we want our first and only one to have the best." I could go on. The four examples given here are sufficient illustrations of how and why attitudes toward money can lead to or reflect critical problems.

Do I make these problems up? I wish I did, and that they never really happen. How vividly I remember the exuberant young couple who were sincerely responsive for virtually everything I proposed in a long series of premarital sessions, until I spoke of money. A glazed look—not hostile, just empty. One year later. Long-distance telephone call. Help needed. "We thought we were the last ones in the world who would ever quarrel over money, but my husband wants to lend money to his father and I don't think he should. Now we're not talking to each other. Apologies for not listening when you talked about money. Can I get my husband on the other line?" They're fine now, fine not merely because they worked through the immediate problem, but because they looked seriously at the whole question of money and marriage. I cite them as but one example of the too-many true stories I could relate, many not working out happily at all. Far better to take that serious look *before* marriage, but it need never be too late.

Money can take on the properties of a living organism, indeed, a cancer, that eats away at love, disrupts harmony, corrodes unity. Obviously, it need not be an evil in itself, but those who love it unduly or use it for power or control or perversely in any way can put their marriages at grave risk. I am well aware, of course, that severe poverty can have a devastating effect on a marriage, as can unemployment and related ills. I see such every day, so I'm not naive about the importance of money. I simply urge that those preparing for marriage and those whose marriages are less than what they had hoped for, look very seriously at what can be friend or foe. After all, if even Christ could be betrayed for thirty pieces of silver, can *anybody* ignore the power of money, even a couple who are absolutely certain nothing can ever betray their love?

16

Being Loved for Oneself

Personality Development in the Religious Life is the rather misleading title of what I find to be a very helpful book by two Jesuit psychologists, Fathers Cristov and Evoy. The title misleads only in that the principles outlined by the author are equally applicable to every walk of life, and not only religious. A bricklayer could profit as could a schoolteacher, a medical doctor as an engineer or a lawyer. Most particularly, I have found the book useful for couples preparing for marriage and for those already married. Regrettably, it is long out of print, so I cherish my copy.

The authors focus on love, on being convinced that one is loved for himself or herself, or at least *lovable*, that is, capable of being loved. The opposite of love, they suggest, is rejection, real or perceived, not merely rejection because of what one has said or done but rejection of one's very self. The tendency of those who believe themselves rejected as *persons* is to counterreject: "I'll get you before you get me." The most positive and constructive force in the world is love; the most negative and destructive is rejection.

What does it all mean? I can never forget the troubled young couple who came to see me almost fifty years ago. Call them Helen and Tom, a handsome couple, indeed, she, a former "beauty queen," blond and statuesque. Their seemingly ideal marriage had begun to deteriorate into bickering, frustration, emptiness. No major visible problems, no infidelity. In due time, however, I learned a great deal.

Helen had been accustomed to adulation from childhood, because of her beauty. Her parents had raved over what a pretty little girl she was; in high school, she was queen of the prom, in college, the "Miss" of her particular state. Tom loved her at first sight and every day thereafter, and for the first several years of their marriage told her so a dozen times a day, always adding a word about her beauty. Then a dozen times became eleven, ten, even fewer, and praise of her beauty was less frequently emphasized. She found herself looking in the mirror more and more, fearing to find even a shadow of a wrinkle, a single graying hair. What was her real concern? *My husband doesn't love me anymore. In fact, he never really loved* me, *he loved only my beauty. Now it's fading and his love is fading with it.* Helen and Tom are real people, not make-believe, and not singular.

In time I learned that Helen had always had such fears. She feared as a child that her parents loved her *only* because they could show her off to others as a beauty. She feared that in high school she was chosen prom queen *only* because of her looks, and on, and on, and on. The key word is "only." *No one truly loves me as a person. People like me because I can sing and dance, because I do anything they want me to do. But if I lose my looks or my talents, or I stop performing as a monkey for an organ grinder, what then?*

If nobody loves me for myself, is it that anybody who sees me beneath the surface, beneath all the appearances and the performances, recognizes that I am actually worthless, indeed, intrinsically evil? Am I, then, intrinsically unlovable, so that it is impossible for anyone really to love me for myself? Round and round it goes, according to Cristov and Evoy (my words, not theirs), until I end up in complete self-loathing, begging to be loved, but terrified lest anyone climb over the wall I have erected around my innermost being, and see me as I really am. So I "counterreject." I never let anyone get too close to the inner me. If anyone begins to penetrate into what I am really like inside, I turn away, even doing something to offend, by way of protecting my "secret" of how bad I really am. How often may this happen in marriage, after a couple begin to "know" each other in a different way?

What a horrifying vicious circle, and what it can do to a marriage. Is there no escape? Are we born that way, or so in the grip of early childhood experiences that we are doomed to a lifetime of believing ourselves incapable of being loved for ourselves, a lifetime of feeling rejected, evil, guilty? Not as long as God is God.

I am well aware that some marriages may need psychological counseling, or even serious psychological or psychiatric therapy. I write as a priest, not as a therapist. I have come to believe, however, that while a competent and responsible therapist can significantly help a marriage or an individual suffering from what I have described briefly above, some people will be "cured" only when they come to recognize that *God* loves them, not *despite* what they are, but *because* of what they are. We cannot be unlovable if someone loves us. But God, who *is* Love, *always* loves us, no matter what we have done or been.

I am not suggesting that prayer is a substitute for needed psychotherapy, any more than it is a substitute for a cast on a broken leg. I am suggesting strongly that whereas therapy can help reveal the origins of the "illness" of feeling rejected as a person, and help us function effectively, until we come to believe that someone loves us for ourselves, our lives will not be what God intended them to be. And I repeat, if we truly come to believe that God loves us for ourselves, then we can no longer convince ourselves that we are incapable of being loved for ourselves.

Is it all theory? In my experience, it is far more. I suggest that many chronic drunks are running always from themselves, or from those they fear will reject them. I suggest the same about those who "protect" themselves with terrible tempers, those who pretend they don't care what anybody thinks about them, those who make themselves look unattractive so they can have an "excuse" for not being loved. Again, it goes on and on and on.

This book is not intended as a short course in "pop" psychology. It is my personal belief, however, born of observation and of years of trying to help individuals and married couples, that an understanding of the power of both love and rejection can be immensely helpful. "Let me kiss it and make it better," many a wise mother has said to many a screaming child with a skinned knee.

I'm sorry the Cristov and Evoy book is out of circulation, but God's love is available without charge.

17

The Frustration-Aggression
Phenomenon

The frustration-aggression phenomenon is a commonplace of every life. Who never gets frustrated? Who, getting frustrated, doesn't have to bite his tongue, or want to kick the cat? What wife is never irked by a husband, what husband by a wife? By being irked, I mean wanting to throw something, for example, although not necessarily at the offending party. It could be a matter of slamming a door to get the annoyance out of your system.

This is only the second time in this book that I have introduced what some might consider curbstone psychology, but I believe a number of psychologists would agree with me that the frustration-aggression phenomenon can damage many a marriage. And the problem is that it can so often disguise itself because it frequently works at the unconscious level. Moreover, the immediate *object* of the aggression, or of the anger, or of what could even be an act of violence, is not necessarily the *cause* of the frustration.

A man works in a pressure-filled job. One morning his boss gives him a hard time about something. He considers himself innocent and wants to argue, or even return the criticism to the boss. But he needs the job. He bites his tongue and seethes with anger all day. Finally he goes home. A child has left a toy on the steps. He picks it up and slams it, then screams at the youngster as though mayhem has been committed. His wife tries to defend the child or to dismiss the child's offense as negligible, or tries to calm her husband down. He turns on her and a battle royal is off and running. Frustration-aggression. As frequently as not, the anger explodes in the "safest" direction. His wife can't fire him, nor can his youngster. But what does he do to both of them by such behavior?

It's a natural enough reaction and usually harmless enough when controlled, but how destructive if given free rein. Indeed, God himself is often the object of anger and bitterness because of a frustration unrelated to God except that, since he knows all things, we demand that he control all things, to prevent bad things from happening to us. No matter that he gives us free will. Nothing matters when we're frustrated enough.

By definition, of course, frustration is a blocking of our will in a way that we can do little about. No matter which way we turn, we're up against a stone wall. A broken leg, a poor complexion, a fire, a job loss, a battle with terminal cancer, death of a husband or wife. The causes of frustration can be trivial or monumental, but the frustration itself, unless recognized for what it is, thought through and prayed through, can lead us to do some very foolish things, indeed, from an act of infidelity, in order to "get even," to suicide or even murder. Child abuse, wife abuse, excessive drinking, drugs, staying away from Mass—the possibilities are incalculable.

Mostly, however, the frustration-aggression phenomenon works in much less dramatic ways and in "little" things. It's the constancy of it, nonetheless, that can corrode a marriage, lessen affection, eat away at love.

It can happen to priests, as well, and to bishops. We can get to feel like functionaries, with phones ringing off the hook, the mail piling up, the bills piling even higher, the demands for personal attention seeming impossible to fulfill, etc. In that respect, the frustration can be quite like that experienced by a husband or wife, a father or mother. Every once in a while a priest blows up, says things he shouldn't say, does things he shouldn't do. Maybe someone in his own family is sick or in trouble; maybe he is experiencing a temptation that won't seem to go away. So he excoriates his congregation, which is completely innocent. A child cries during his homily, and he goes into a tirade totally disproportionate to the minor interruption. He lets off steam. Frustration-aggression: the human condition.

I write about it here, however, because in my experience in helping couples to prepare for marriage, or in meeting with couples whose marriages are floundering, I find so many people who have never even heard of the "frustration-aggression equation." They don't recognize why one or the other party is so edgy, so easily provoked, seemingly always angry, especially when they know they have at least consciously done nothing to cause the aggression. Once they learn that they are neither the real cause nor the real object of the anger, they can weather the storm and help the other party to work through the problem. As with everything worthwhile, it can take time, patience, and prayer, but even the *knowledge* of what's wrong can be an important step toward a solution.

18

Reality Check

I had only ever seen them in church. He was always tilted back as far as his wheelchair would allow, eyes closed. She stood behind him, ever dabbing gently at the corners of his mouth with a tissue, hiking him back into the wheelchair whenever he would slide forward. He was clearly older than she by a number of years. On my way to the altar, I would always pause to give him a blessing and call him *friend*. He seemed aware of my presence; she was always thrilled, because she loves him.

I didn't know their names until one day she called me at my office, frantic, from a hospital. He seemed to be moments from death. Could I come and anoint him? At that very moment I was caught in another emergency, but my priest associate went gladly and immediately. I followed as soon as I could. He seemed significantly improved. Then she told me the story and showed me the newspaper clippings about this utterly helpless man and herself. It is its own Pastoral Letter on Marriage.

Famous people from every walk of life posed with her husband in the pictures in the clippings, few better known than her husband and herself. I was inexpressibly shocked to see the two of them, an internationally acclaimed dance team, gliding with indescribable grace in ballrooms throughout the world, on stages, in their own studios, where they taught other professionals. The pictures show him tall, supple, handsome, while she is a vision of loveliness. For forty romantic years they danced together, finally closing their act one night some twenty years ago in the beautiful ballroom of the Waldorf-Astoria hotel. He is paralyzed now and has Alzheimer's. She tends him in every way, and feeds him and cleans him and loves him.

I don't want to sermonize on this loveliest of love stories. It is too exquisite for the clumsiness of words. I simply offer it here as a brief insert by way of a "reality check" against what I have been saying in the book about love, sacrifice, and communion in marriage in the Lord.

There is little chance that the glamour magazines will feature this couple as their Christmas valentine this year, but if this book were to be published as a photo story, I would want them on the front cover—not as they were, but as they are.

Parenting

19

A Few Modest Questions
for Parents

According to a report of a recent survey, "adults think much
of the blame" for young people's attitudes (ages 5 to 17),
"rests with their parents." The survey is called "Kids These
Days: What Americans Really Think About the Next Genera-
tion." It was conducted by *Public Agenda* and reported in
Catholic New York, July 10, 1997. I suspect it is fairly typical of
what large numbers of people think. I remember reading a
book years ago, *History Begins at Sumer*. It described life in
the third millennium before Christ, in part of Babylonia,
modern southern Iraq. It excoriated fathers for the behavior
of their sons. An ancient practice, indeed.

But is it all that simple? In a culture drenched with materi-
alism, secularism, pornography, drugs, violence, glorification
of sex, ridicule of marriage, highly paid, widely publicized icons
of promiscuity, filthy rock lyrics, is there a tougher job in the
world today than trying to rear children? This chapter is in no
way intended to add to the criticism of parents. On the contrary, it is intended to offer a few *very* gentle suggestions by
way of a few *very* modest questions.

Obviously, since children are not machines, there are no
"check-off" lists for parents to follow to assure "running order." No buttons can be pushed to "access" a child. No levers
pulled, no switches turned. But there *are* questions that par-

ents can ask themselves. This chapter will raise some, by no means all, of these questions. Let's start at the beginning.

When parents bring a baby for baptism, the priest or deacon asks, "What name do you give your child?" That places the responsibility quite squarely. This is the name this child will carry for life. Have you given prayerful thought to the name of a saint or of Mary for your child's protection throughout life, and to serve as a model in a world in which models are so desperately needed?

So often I hear parents speculating before birth on what they might call a child. They cite names of movie or TV celebrities, sports figures, names they just happen to like, even though they have no particular meaning. Whatever happened to the saints, to those who have gone before us and shown us the way, ordinary people who lived extraordinary lives, even if poor or unknown?

I can understand, of course, when parents want to give a family name to a child. Wasn't Archbishop Fulton J. Sheen's mother's maiden name Fulton? I believe so. Even then, however, a saint's name can be included, whatever a child is actually called in the future.

I might make another point here that I make during premarital discussions. So often I have seen grandparents hurt that, although they may have many grandchildren, none are named after their grandparents. This can be a tricky thing, of course, especially where there are two sets of living grandparents. It may not be a critical issue, but then, many marriages suffer far more from a piling up of little issues than by even a single critical issue.

Why do I make so much of this? Only that a child may have a model and protector? That's primary, but there's another reason. It suggests to the child, it seems to me, that his or her parents took their faith seriously, and that maybe that's a good idea. The same is true in the selection of godparents. Are they the kind of people who really care about the child's spiritual future? What example will they give by their lives?

This brings up the issue of parental example, in general, and a host of related questions. What kind of religious life do children see parents leading? Any signs of prayer: before and after meals, at bedtime, in the morning? Regular Mass attendance? Periodic confession? Are youngsters taught the rosary and given one to carry? Do they ever see a religious medal around a parent's neck? Do the parents know the parish priest? Do they involve themselves and children in the work or activities of the parish? Do they teach children to support the parish financially? Isn't it all part of growing up Catholic?

What kind of language is heard in the home? The language of love or the language of bickering and divisiveness and anger? Is the language crude and obscene, or is it respectful? Can children see affection and understanding between their parents? Unspoken evidence of willing sacrifice for each other? What do children see parents watching on television? Is that perhaps even more important than what children themselves might watch? What guidelines are children given? What do they learn by example?

Bad example can be such a boomerang. Who doesn't know parents who, in the presence of their children, criticize or ridicule or show complete indifference to their own parents? What happens when children are given this example growing up? Do they treat their parents the same way they saw their own grandparents treated? What a magnificent effect on children is the example of parents who take care of their own parents as they age, become ill, lonely, in need. Many parents have sacrificed a great deal to bring one or the other of their own widowed parents into their home for extended periods. What a wonderful example to their own children. Obviously, such arrangements are not always possible or even appropriate. It may be better for everyone for an aged or infirm parent to be in a nursing home, to receive the care required. In those cases, then, it benefits children to be taken to visit a grandparent, to help in little ways, to know that their parents have not forgotten their *own* parents.

There's nothing earth-shattering in any of this. It's homespun stuff, all of it, but the stuff of things that I have seen in family after family over the course of many years. So often when we try to help a couple prepare for marriage, it's almost as though we expect the *two* of them, *alone,* to live happily ever after. But marriage is not only for love; it's for children. Sounds prosaic, but yet it can be all too easy to forget. As easy as it can be to forget that no individual marries another individual who has emerged out of thin air. Each of us is from a family—whether a traditional family, a single-parent family, a living family, a family deceased. We have been shaped by our families, for good or for bad. We have obligations to our families, to lesser or greater degrees. Families expect things of us, some less, some more. It is a *rare* individual who is completely unentangled. It is a *foolish* individual who believes that the mere words, "I'm marrying you, not your family," change anything at all.

Nothing asked or stated above will make it dramatically easier for newlyweds or older parents to prepare their children to live truly Catholic lives in a truly hostile world. But with God's grace and a lot of prayers it may help in an immensely difficult task.

20

Transmitters
of Spiritual Life

Long before any priest was called Monsignor or Cardinal, he was called Father. In earliest times, bishops were called fathers. Priests hearing sacramental confessions were called fathers. The word "abbot" used for the head of a Benedictine or other abbey was a derivative of "abba," father.

Which has what to do with marriage, since most priests are not married? In early sections of this book I spoke of the many similarities between the sacrament of matrimony and the sacrament of holy orders. Immanuel Cardinal Suhard, some sixty years ago archbishop of Paris, said that the priest receives the sacrament of holy orders because it is he who must bring spiritual order into the disordered world. Think of how utterly chaotic the world would be without marriage. Look at how chaotic it *is* where marriage is spurned, fidelity is ridiculed, sex without marriage is accepted as the norm, children are deprived of family life.

The proudest title of any priest, whatever "ecclesiastical" honors are given him, is surely *Father.* The pope is called pope because he is the "papa," the father, our Holy Father. "Father" was the title I looked forward to as a seminarian, before ordination, not because it would bring status or prestige, and certainly not because I expected to lord it over men and women years my senior (or over any others). I saw the priest as father because he transmitted spiritual life to those given into his care. Obviously, he was only the instrument, the channel used in a special way by the giver of all life, the Father who is our God.

It is in this capacity, as transmitter of spiritual life, that I see a striking relationship between the priest and a married couple. While physical procreation is one of the primary purposes and priorities of marriage, the ensuing obligation to feed and clothe and generally care for the physical needs of children is clear; and with the transmission of physical life goes the grave responsibility to transmit spiritual life.

Who must be the first teacher about God and that God is Love, except parents? Who best teaches an infant to pray, to make the Sign of the Cross? Who, quite apart from formal teaching, gives the first evidence of faith and hope and love, by the very nature of their lives, than parents? Who but parents must be the first to teach children, "Fear not those who can harm the body, but those who can cast both body and soul into hell"? Or who, by example, must be the first to teach the first commandment and the second: to love the Lord our God with our whole minds and our whole souls and all our strength and our neighbors as ourselves? Who is a wife's most immediate neighbor, if not her husband; a husband's, if not his wife?

Am I simply being sentimental and "pious"? On the contrary, I am being thoroughly realistic. "As the twig is bent, so grows the elm tree." What greater privilege could be given a priest, what more awesome responsibility, than the care of souls? Can we even begin to guess the "blinding value" of the soul? Has our culture so eroded our very sense of being human, that it seems quaint to speak of our immortal souls?

Is it possible that our culture has so strongly emphasized physical health and material success that parents come to consider their *primary* responsibility toward their children to focus on these as the "be-all and end-all" of parenthood? Not that I would therefore underestimate either the good will or the self-sacrifice practiced by countless numbers of parents who do focus on the health and success of their children. Who can question the grave importance of this focus? But if we truly believe that the fundamental purpose for our existence is to come to know and to love and to serve God in this world, and to be happy with Him forever in heaven, should this not be transmitted to children as enormously important? Should it not be intermingled with every experience of their lives from infancy?

Another way of asking the question: What makes a parent proud of a child? That the child can sing and dance or recite poetry? That a child has golden hair or beautiful skin? Is a promising athlete, a potential doctor, lawyer, research scientist? Or is a parent proud of all such achievements, but far more: that a child has learned the worth of the human soul? Does a child demonstrate a sense of prayerfulness, of love of God and neighbor, of gratitude for the great gift of faith?

It seems to this unmarried "Father" that parents can make the same well-meaning mistakes in regard to their children as to one another. Earlier in this book we noted that the sheer demands of making a living can gradually estrange a husband from wife, a wife from a husband. Both may be working hard to pay the rent or the mortgage, to save for children's education, to pay the premiums on healthcare insurance, etc., etc., etc. A couple may scarcely see each other, much less have "quality time" together. Even excessive volunteerism in the best of causes can have a similar result. Who hasn't seen how a couple can drift apart, with time for everything and everyone except for each other? Can not the same be true in regard to their children?

I write as a priest, a Father, who happens to be at the same time the bishop of a huge and immensely complex archdiocese. The administrative and financial responsibilities are heavy. The cost of failure could be devastating for our schools, our healthcare facilities, our charitable activities. But if in the midst of it all, I have no time for God's people, no time to teach and to preach the Gospel, to celebrate Mass, to visit the sick, to bury the dead—to simply *love* those souls in my care—what kind of priest or bishop am I? What kind of "Father"? Yet it can happen to all of us, single or married, priest, mother or father, that we can't see the forest for the trees; we risk not seeing the needs of the soul when we focus on virtually everything else. I can sympathize with parents because I have the same problem—and I don't even have to get kids to Little League games.

It's not easy for any of us, anymore than it was for Mary and Joseph. It's sobering to remind ourselves that when they thought they had lost the Christ Child, they searched day and night without sleep; it's clear that life would never have been the same for them had they not found Him. And where did they find Him? In the Temple. Is Jesus saying something about every child's need?

21

Would You Want Your Son to Be Just Like You?

The title startled me as it came across the car radio: "Runaway fathers, throwaway kids." I believe it was the commercial for a CBS radio program, and it had a special impact on me because I was at that very moment thinking of Father's Day.

I don't know the "Promise Keepers" movement except by way of media reports, but if its goal is to help men be better husbands and fathers, I'm grateful. The Lord knows how tough it is to be a good husband and father in our culture. I'm not speaking of the physical "runaways" who "throw away" their kids. They are hardly likely to read this book. I'm speaking of those who stay right at home, but abandon their kids morally and spiritually. It's frighteningly easy to do. Indeed, it takes a concerted effort not to do it. It takes time, thought, prayer, and, above all, courage, not to.

How can fathers abandon their kids, even while physically present to them? Simply by going along with the culture. One could see signs of it some thirty years ago or more. It became difficult to distinguish between father and son in styles of haircuts and clothing, except that the father looked sillier. Kids began setting the pace and the pattern. As recently as ten years ago, when I preached about the harmful effects of a lot of hard rock music, by way of both sounds and lyrics, I was roundly excoriated by fathers who liked it as much as their sons and daughters; laughed at the "pot" smoking, if they did not, indeed, join in.

The devaluation of fatherhood has been a stock-in-trade of our modern culture, from comic strips depicting "cave men" as predictably stupid brutes, dragging their wives by the hair with one hand, wielding a massive club in the other, all the way to the ooh's and ah's over "hunks" bare-chested to prove the manly prowess of pectoral muscles! Periodically the nonsense becomes "theological": "In the name of the Father and of the Son and of the Holy Spirit." becomes "In the name of the Creator, and of the Redeemer and of the Sanctifier," if you please.

The conspiracy against fatherhood ranges from the most radical form of machoism, such as the idolatry accorded a male athlete who boasts of the number of women who have slept with him, to the most radical form of feminism that would leave Freud himself scratching his head in bewilderment. This is to say nothing, of course, of the men's shirts and jeans and underwear ads, the movie and television idols interviewed on big-time talk shows trying to prove, not *evolution*, but *devolution*, that any man truly gifted by nature can become hairier than any ape. Are young boys, young men, immune from all this? Do they see their fathers almost literally "aping" such folly, or, at least, laughing along, failing to reflect the slightest revulsion?

Countless numbers of parents make indescribable sacrifices for their kids, working almost unbelievable numbers of hours to provide for them, particularly to assure a college education. How many, however, are bewildered by what their youngsters are taught or not taught in college, or which values prevail and which are ridiculed. Many parents awe me by what they do for their kids, but I am saddened by the way their best efforts can be undermined by the culture. Who *says* kids have to go to Florida on Easter breaks? Who *says* high schoolers have to have sophisticated graduation proms and all-night parties? Talk to high-school principals who try to curb some of these activities and they'll tell you that some parents become their worst enemies. "Who do you think you are, telling my own son or daughter what to do?" Sadly, in too many cases honesty would compel them to add: "I, myself, never tell them what to do." Oscar Wilde's silly maxim is, indeed, taken more seriously in our culture than we might like to believe: "Fathers should be neither seen or heard. That is the only proper basis for married life."

As I am neither husband nor father, it's easy for me to talk, I know. And I know, too, that I might well do a miserable job as either. I ask no one to listen to me, however, but rather to the Lord: "Would any of you fathers give your son a snake when he asks for a fish…a scorpion when he asks for an egg?" (Lk 11:11–12). Or when he says to Job: "Stand up now like a man and answer the questions I ask you" (38:3). Aren't an awful lot of kids looking to their fathers to give them not what they, the kids, think they want, but what their fathers believe is best for them? Don't countless numbers of kids want their fathers to be real men, not machos, but men who stand up to the culture, instead of being overwhelmed by it? What did our Lord ask the people about John the Baptist: "What did you go out into the desert to see, a reed shaken by the wind, a man clothed in soft garments?…Yet I tell you no man born of woman is greater than John the Baptist." Unless, perhaps, Jesus might have added, Joseph, my foster father, that "just man."

I have often asked myself: "If you had a son, would you want him to be just like you? If not, why not?" Once again, it's an easy question for me to ask, but if I had the responsibility, it would be a tough question to answer. One of my greatest privileges as a priest and as archbishop of New York, however, is to meet on a daily basis and to have come to know in a personal way countless numbers of fathers about whom I could answer without the slightest hesitation: "Would you want your son to be just like them?" The answer? "Thank God, I certainly would."

22

Teachable Moments

No pastoral letter ever written by a bishop, no encyclical by a pope, can teach a child as can a parent. With due respect, while such documents can give wonderful guidance to parents and should certainly be studied, it is safe to assume that few babies ever learned to bless themselves with the Sign of the Cross, or ever learned to lisp a prayer, by reading a pastoral letter or an encyclical.

Following the baptism of a baby, in the new rite, come special blessings for first, the mother, then the father. The one for the father reads: "He and his wife will be the first teachers of their child in the ways of faith. May they also be the best of teachers, bearing witness to the faith by what they say and do, in Christ Jesus our Lord."

"By what they say and do." When I baptize, I give to the father or godfather of the infant the lighted candle used in the ceremony, the candle symbolizing Christ, the Light of the World, and the duty of the Christian to bring the light of Christ to others. I offer it to the parents to take home, and suggest that they might want to light it on the anniversary of the spiritual birthday, the day of baptism, as families often light candles on a cake on the date of the physical birthday, and, when the child can understand, to explain why. I often wonder how many parents do this or just think me an old sentimentalist for suggesting it.

But such "teachable moments" can make a tremendous difference in a child's spiritual future, to say nothing of the spiritual here-and-now for the couple themselves. So much is in these little things: teaching rudimentary prayers, as the Sign of the Cross and such. (I still bow my head at the name of Jesus, because I was so taught when I was about six months old, I suspect, even though it's no longer "in.") Didn't my parents get a lot out of teaching me such things, including the sense of awe I developed over time in regard to holy things and holy people and holy places?

Throughout these pages I have been comparing marriage with the priesthood. One of the most crucial responsibilities of the priest is to teach, to teach in his preaching, to teach in whatever he says and writes outside the pulpit, to teach by priestly example. Is this not true of parents, this indispensable requirement to teach their children by word and example? What a responsibility, but what a privilege.

As a priest forever preaching, speaking, and writing, I find myself enriched by preparations required for every homily, every lecture, every article I write. I must study, read and reread the sacred Scriptures and commentaries on the Scriptures, pore through papal encyclicals, the traditions of the Church, appropriate secular literature, and on, and on, and on. My own spiritual life is deepened, reinforced, enhanced, in preparing and in preaching *to* others, in writing *for* others. And in integrity, I must ask myself constantly how seriously I am trying to practice what I preach. How many souls have been alienated, faith weakened or shattered, trust destroyed, when a priest fails to reflect his own preaching, and engages in scandalous behavior. How the credibility of *all* priests falls into question when but a few betray their trust.

Is the priesthood singular in this regard? What happens to the faith, the trust, the hope of children who see their parents engage in or somehow condone lascivious behavior, demonstrate infidelity, one to the other, treat each other with bitterness or contempt? How many children grow in faith and learn to practice it devoutly for the rest of their lives if their parents are lukewarm or nonpracticing? If some young potential vocations to the priesthood are lost because of the bad example of a local priest, how many young women or men fear or distrust entering into marriage because of what they have seen in their own parents? How many young women are skeptical about all men, how many young men are cynical about all women because of what may have been actually *taught* by a mother or father, respectively?

Years ago I was sitting in a living room and happened to glance at the face of a little girl as she overheard her mother saying that she, the little girl, had been an "accident." A contraceptive had failed. The child was devastated. I have since watched that little girl grow into young womanhood. For years she considered herself worthless, and behaved accordingly. Thank God, she has since found a love that has literally saved her from a lifetime of deterioration.

Children aren't stupid. How many are well aware that their parents practice artificial contraception, and recognize that either they, themselves, could have been "accidents," or believe that their parents must not prize children very highly? How does that affect their own future marriages and attitudes toward children? And quite apart from the question of children, or even the question of morality, what does artificial contraception do to married love, to intimacy, to the spiritual union, the sacramental oneness we have been discussing in this book?

I am convinced that many couples engage habitually in the practice for what they consider to be the best of motives. For example, they want the "best" for their children; hence, they severely limit the number. They want the "best" education, housing, healthcare plan, and so forth. I understand this. But I don't believe that such couples, despite their good intentions, realize the price their marriage is paying, or the price the child or children they do have may ultimately pay. Could one of the reasons they don't realize this be that we priests too often don't talk about it in marriage preparation, or in homilies, or, perhaps, in the confessional? If so, our silence surely does not serve the couples we are ordained to serve, or their children. Moreover, if we priests fail to address this issue because we believe people will "turn us off," we can be gravely underestimating both their fundamental goodness and potential. The "world" tells them all about the value of contraceptives. They are starved, sometimes unconsciously, to hear about pure love and sacrifice, self-discipline and its value in marriage.

Children are, indeed, God's wonderful gift in marriage. The philosopher-poet Goethe gives us a provocative reminder: "If you treat a child as he is, he will remain as he is. If you treat a child as though he were what he could be and should be, the child will become what he could be and should be." Goethe used the masculine pronoun, but would be the last to exclude little girls or young women from his maxim. He had too much respect for them to do that. Nor would he exclude married couples.

What Makes
a Marriage
Not a
Marriage

23

Nullity of Marriage— Regardless of Appearances

How often could it happen? Once in ten million marriages? God knows. Once was horrifying enough for Mary and John. They had been married for ten years. Beautiful wedding witnessed by a close-friend priest. Childless, but pillars of the parish. A wonderful story because each had been reared in an orphanage on opposite sides of the country, and had met only in their twenties.

For Mary and John to learn ten years after their wedding day that they were blood brother and sister was devastating. They separated quietly, with the parish shocked, but not knowing the cause. Some time later each married another, in Church. Former parishioners who learned of their second marriages were scandalized. How could it be? What's the Church coming to?

Their "marriage," of course, was null and void from the beginning. The Church was not permitting them to "remarry" after a civil divorce. The Church was simply saying: "It is impossible for a brother and sister to enter into a valid marriage with each other." Each party is therefore free to marry someone else.

Is this an extreme case? Of course. Does it justify the Church's running a "divorce mill"? Were the Church running a "divorce mill," an extreme case would certainly not justify it, nor would any other. But is the Church really operating a "divorce mill"? Is what we call the Marriage Tribunal process simply a euphemistic term for getting permission to remarry following divorce? Or, equally bad, is it true that if you have enough money or influence you can get an annulment, no matter what kind of marriage you have? First question: No. Second question: No. Third question: No. *Regardless of the appearances.*

Which takes me back to the extreme case I cited above: the question of *appearances.* Mary and John *appeared* to be validly married. They loved each other. They entered into marriage with the best intentions in the world. They were under no pressure, no force; they did not marry out of fear. They were mature and well balanced, with apparently everything going for them. Ten years later they still loved each other, with no significant ruptures in their relations. When they divorced and each remarried, the Church *appeared* to be violating its own teaching and sacred Scripture: "What God has joined together, let no man split asunder." But it was all in the *appearances*, and, as quite often, the Church had to keep silent, unable or unwilling out of charity to tell the world the true story.

Should the Church have told the world that Mary and John were brother and sister? Should the Church have given the couple a "dispensation" to "stay married"? Of course not. The Church can not declare any couple married if there is a dire impediment—an intrinsic obstacle. A sister and brother simply *cannot* validly marry. The most the Church could do would be to declare on the evidence available that the marriage was null and void from the beginning.

I repeat that this was an extreme case; but the principle is virtually the same in every case in which the Church, upon thorough investigation at the request of either party, tries to judge objectively, on the basis of evidence, the *initial* validity or invalidity of a marriage. In other words, did a true and valid marriage take place in every sense of the term at the very outset? It is not a question of *appearances,* or even of the goodness and the intentions of the couple, alone. The question is one of fact: Were there any hidden dire impediments; or, in reverse, were all the requirements of a true and valid marriage present? The Church does not imply bad will or moral fault on the part of either party. The Church simply looks for the facts, to the degree that these are humanly discernible. If the facts involve psychological elements, psychologists or psychiatrists are consulted; if the facts involve medical elements, medical doctors are consulted.

It is only after such a process that the Church declares its finding: that in the Church's judgment a marriage is valid, or that it is null and void from the beginning. *But the presumption must always be in favor of the marriage.* There can be no "maybes" involved: *Maybe* one or the other party wasn't mature; *maybe* one or the other party was forced, etc. The Tribunal process must be a sincere effort to both get at the truth and to offer peace of conscience where possible. "The truth will make you free."

The Tribunal process is intended, however, to address exceptions, no matter how many they may be. The "rule" is that marriage is unbreakable. Every effort must be made, all help must be offered, to "make a marriage work." Nor does the Tribunal process offer the option for nullification simply because marriages aren't working. The process investigates the situation prior to and at the time of the exchange of marriage consent, to discern validity or invalidity from the outset of the marriage.

Is the process perfect? Far from it, since it's a human process. Is it subject to abuse? Unquestionably. Those conducting the process could be too permissive, or too excessive. In my personal experience, there is generally an honest effort to dot all the i's and cross all the t's, and yet to carry out an apostolate of true compassion and deserved peace.

Are there unanswered questions? Many. One of the most difficult coming from individuals who have been involuntarily divorced by a spouse is to have the Church declare their marriage null and void without their consent. That can be terribly hard. In reality, however, once an investigative process has begun, at the behest of either party, what can the Church say but: "This is what we find. This marriage has been valid from the beginning, this one has not." An appeal process is built into the Tribunal system. The Church requires that it be followed, whatever the outcome of the initial investigation.

In a succeeding section I will try to address further misunderstandings. Confusion and pain are far too widespread to be ignored. Too many good people are asking: "What has happened to the Church? I was always taught that if you were married in Church, you were married once and for all, for better or for worse." And except when we are speaking of *appearances*, rather than reality, they are right. And even with the options of the Tribunal process, the discovery of an *initial* dire impediment does not necessarily mean that parties must or should separate, or that it is too late for them to exchange marriage consent, and be married without doubt, "once and for all," until death do them part. As we'll discuss in the next section.

24

"Marriage Cases"

When I was a young priest, what today we call "marriage cases" were a rarity, at least in the experience of the average priest. I'm speaking of the mid to late 40's. We were accustomed to young couples who had eloped, married before a justice of the peace, then came to have their civil marriages validated by the priest, most frequently encouraged by their parents. These were not "marriage cases."

Our "cases" would usually be those involving a Catholic who had married "outside the Church," that is, before a minister or justice of the peace, then divorced, and who now wanted to marry someone in the Church. We called these "lack or defect of form" cases, because the "form" required was a sacramental marriage, and that normally had to take place between a priest and two witnesses. Or we might have a case of a Catholic's wanting to marry someone of a non-Christian religion who had been divorced and converted to Catholicism. A few other types of cases might have confronted us, as well, but they were relatively few in number and we usually referred them to the diocesan chancery office or to the Marriage Tribunal, depending on the case itself.

While many wonderful and enduring marriages were entered into during World War II, for many the war seems to have been a turning point, as for our culture in general. Great numbers of hasty marriages took place during the war as hundreds of thousands of men were drafted, and quickly left for the war zone. Many marriages took place, as well, between virtual strangers. A young man, hardly more than a boy, from somewhere else might meet a girl at a shipping-out point. Neither had any real knowledge of the other's background, convictions, or ideas about marriage. Moved by a mix of patriotism, the pseudo-romance of war, and a sense of pity, a priest might be moved to witness such a marriage without adequate investigation and with no real premarital instructions. Large numbers of young men and women sowed the wind and reaped the whirlwind. The postwar situation was turbulent for many.

Perhaps the psychological and cultural upheavals that took place during and after World War II have never been adequately studied, or at least fully understood. Men moved from small towns into major cities, engaged in experiences and events previously unimagined. Women went into war production factories; Rosie the Riveter became nationally famous. Other wars would follow before the country settled down—Korea, Vietnam. The entire "establishment" was shaken. Nothing seemed permanent, reliable, or predictable.

In the meanwhile, the drug culture was developing, movies and television were reweaving attitudes toward the family, sexual morality, and premarital sexual relations. Contraception became a way of life. It was all too much, and with the rampant confusion born of gross misunderstandings of the intentions, the work, and the actual documents of the Second Vatican Council (massively unread), many young Catholics in particular simply lost their moorings. They no longer felt secure in what or whom to believe. Suddenly the whole world of marriage and family seemed to be falling apart, and divorce the rule, rather than the exception.

Is there any wonder that the number of "marriage cases" exploded, or that appeals for declarations of nullity based on alleged emotional immaturity or psychological instability began flooding marriage tribunals? Catholics are not unaffected by the general culture. The day is long gone since Hollywood star and "America's Sweetheart," Mary Pickford, had to stop making movies because of a divorce. It had become completely respectable to be divorced, ridiculous to remain in an "unhappy" marriage, "unfair" to children to subject them to marital disputes. Divorce became a "human right." The option to marry someone else following a divorce likewise became a "human right."

How was the Church to respond to all this? With dignity, patience, understanding, compassion, but firm fidelity to divine teaching: "What God has joined together, let no one split asunder." Every case would have to be examined on the merits, to discern to the degree humanly possible whether from the very beginning *this* marriage was valid or not. Hence the detailed questioning, investigations, medical and psychological evaluations, judgments of witnesses, and most of all the testimony of both spouses when humanly possible.

The Church has had to educate and train large numbers of individuals skilled in marriage law and many related fields. Cases must go through not one but two Church marriage courts and a substantial number must still go to the Holy See. Many people clamor for greater speed in processing cases. Others see the process as bureaucratic or an intrusion into privacy. The Church has a solemn obligation to get at the truth. Perhaps, indeed, the ultimate human right is the right to truth.

In these few pages I have simply attempted to explain some

of the reasons why "marriage cases" have multiplied and why the process can be long, arduous, and complex. In another section I will address some of the specific problems individuals may encounter in respect to the entire issue of a declaration of nullity. But it is good, I think, to reflect on the complexities of this culture in which the Church must "live and move and have its being." There have been less turbulent days in our land.

25

Appeals to
the Marriage Tribunal

M y directions to the Marriage Tribunal of the Archdiocese of New York are simple and straightforward:

1. Treat every soul the same as every other soul, rich
   or poor, powerful or powerless.
2. Go exactly by the book *(The Code of Canon Law)*,
   cutting no corners.
3. Look at the work of the Tribunal as an apostolate of
   justice, of mercy, of compassion, of picking up the
   pieces of broken lives, of deepening faith, offering
   hope, bringing peace.
4. No one is to be deprived of the Tribunal process or
   have a judgment withheld because he or she is unable to make the customary offering (approximately
   $800).

Of the "hate mail" I receive, few letters distress me as do
those alleging that "money talks"—that the rich and powerful
can have a marriage dissolved, a "Church divorce," a declaration of nullity, no matter what the circumstances. The poor al-
legedly have to live with their mistakes. The charge distresses
me because those who make it believe it is true. Why is that?

Obviously, some make the charge out of hostility toward
the Church. They are uninterested in facts. Others make the

charge out of ignorance, often born of something they have read in the newspaper. Ordinary cases of poor and middle-class people don't make headlines. The cases of wealthy people often do. In the Archdiocese of New York in a recent year, for example, the Marriage Tribunal issued declarations of nullity in 670 cases. Those able to make the ordinary offering of $800 did so. Those who could not did not. I do not know of a single case that made the newspapers. (In the United States in 1996, there were more than 50,000 declarations of nullity issued. How many cases made the newspapers? How many were rich and powerful?)

Why, incidentally, is there any contribution or fee at all, $800, $1,200, whatever? Isn't this the Church? Why isn't it free? But who pays the typists for the great amount of documentation that must be prepared? Who pays medical or psychological consultants? Who takes care of travel costs for interviews, office costs, the basics—light, heat, etc? The fact is that, in keeping fees so low, the Archdiocese of New York pays the difference between the real cost and the contribution asked.

There are still others who have problems, however, who are neither hostile toward the Church nor ignorant, but puzzled. I don't blame them. When I was a young priest, a declaration of nullity was rarely heard of. As recently as 1968 there were only 450 in the entire United States. How radically the entire culture seems to have changed, and although Church teaching remains constant, it must be applied to marriages that are often the products of a culture in which psychological immaturity seems commonplace and the notion that *anything can be permanent and indissoluble seems to some like science fiction.*

I don't blame people either for asking such questions as: "How can we be married for twenty-five years, with four children, and suddenly my husband (wife), having met someone else, can be judged to have been psychologically too immature to have entered into a 'true' and permanent marriage with me twenty-five years ago?" That's a question that can be answered in some cases, not all, but it's never easy to answer. Or, "How am I going to tell my kids they are illegitimate, because their father (mother) and I were never really married." Answer: "You don't have to tell them that, because it's not true. You were civilly married. Your children are quite legitimate. There are other, equally difficult questions raised, all understandable.

One of the concerns that pains me very much is that expressed by a disillusioned wife or husband facing an unwanted declaration of nullity requested by the other spouse: "I thought that if I married a Catholic, my marriage would be forever." Sometimes I wonder if some couples live together without marriage because they see even Catholic marriages dissolved. Is anything sacred?

We can't kid ourselves. We of the Church must put far more time, energy, thought, and prayer into preparing for marriage and nourishing marriages than we sometimes do. And the Marriage Tribunal process, even though it is safeguarded by both a review and an appeal procedure, must be carried out with great respect for the sanctity of marriage, the rights of both parties, and careful respect for Church law. It is not surprising that periodically our Holy Father personally addresses the questions that arise and that what are called the Signatura and the Roman Rota scrupulously monitor the cases that are processed throughout the world. We should not dissemble.

Many a priest and bishop worries about the number of declarations in the Church today.

At the same time, the Church is our Mother. She lives by the divine power of the Holy Spirit, while her members are human and can err in their judgments. As a loving mother, she must be faithful to the truth while compassionate toward the wounded.

Let it always be understood, however, that recourse to a civil divorce and appeal to a Marriage Tribunal for a declaration of nullity must yet be the rarest exception. For better, for worse, for richer, for poorer, in sickness and in health, until death must always be the norm.

26

Divorce and Remarriage

How quickly I again become a quivering little boy whenever I receive a letter that begins "How dare you?" I had a fifth-grade teacher who would address me that way periodically in front of the entire class. I always knew that the next question would be "Who do you think you are?" Both questions shriveled me by at least five inches, particularly since I didn't know the answer. All I knew was that I had done something inexcusably shameful, unutterably arrogant, sinister to the core, and that somebody would be sure to tell my mother.

Indeed, when the latest "How dare you" letter arrived, I must confess I put it aside for several days after reading the opening question. It took me that long to grow up again. Only then did I learn that I had been judged guilty of grave scandal by inviting to lunch a couple who had married after each had divorced a previous spouse.

Together with the letter taking me to task came a puzzled one enclosing a newspaper clipping and asking my opinion. The clipping was headlined: "Vatican: Divorced Catholics Who Remarry Should Shun Sex." The story was based on guidelines issued by the Holy See's Pontifical Council on the Family. The questioner asked me sincerely: "Do they [the Pontifical Council] believe two people of the opposite sex can cohabitate, remarry, and live as celibates?" Let us reflect on these issues.

First, the *couples* I lunched with, for there were two couples, one happily married in the Church for some forty years. The other couple seemed to me to be very devout in their own faith. Even were they not, however, should a priest not lunch with them, privately or publicly? Our Lord seemed to be thoroughly nondiscriminatory in regard to those he ate and drank with, like Levi, the tax-collector, who was to become Matthew the apostle, and Zacchaeus, the short man who was in the same business. Some of the women Christ associated with had quite colorful reputations. Jesus not only turned no one away, he went out looking for those in trouble.

Indeed, I have lunched with many a couple quite validly married and with impeccable reputations–some in highly prestigious positions–whose moral and spiritual lives are in shambles. That's a large part of what a priest is all about. Which brings us to the document published by the Pontifical Council for the Family, of which I am a member.

"In many countries," the document notes, "divorce has become a real social 'plague.' Statistics indicate a continuing increase of failures, even among those united in the sacrament of matrimony." Obviously, it goes on to say, the Church cannot remain silent as families are destroyed and divorce becomes a taken-for-granted custom in society.

The divorced may not enter into another marriage unless their previous marriage has been declared null and void by the Church. Catholics who are divorced and remarry without such a declaration of nullity of a previous marriage may not receive holy Communion. This is the unequivocal teaching of the Church. Despite confusion, misunderstanding, and teaching to the contrary, the Church's position has not changed.

Does this mean, however, that a divorced individual or couple in an unlawful or invalid marriage with another is simply to be abandoned? Are they "out of the Church," as some believe, never supposed to darken the door of the Church again? Far from it. The *need* the holy sacrifice of the Mass as much as any of us. And they are welcomed a thousand times over, even though they are forbidden the sacraments until their situation is regularized. As the Council document urges, they must take the steps necessary for spiritual healing, beginning with the recognition of "their irregular situation, which involves a state of sin" and asking God "for the grace of a true conversion."

A major problem in our culture, of course, is that divorce and remarriage have become so common that even some Catholics have come to think of it as a "human right" and consider the Church cruel and unthinking. This is terribly sad for many reasons, not the least of which is that often such individuals or couples don't even want to explore the possibility of having their marriage validated. It's sad, too, because no priest worth his salt ever wants to inflict unnecessary pain. He exists to help people pick up the broken pieces of their lives. His is Christ's own "ministry of reconciliation." It is not his role to denounce *any* sinner. It is for him to denounce sin and only sin. His is the obligation and the privilege to be merciful and compassionate, always telling people the truth as the Church sees it, but gently and lovingly urging them to do whatever they must to be restored to the sacraments.

Is it possible for a married couple to live as celibates, as the second letter-writer cited above asked me? With God's grace, *all* things are possible. Is it possible for someone who is divorced and remarried to live in what we used to call a "brother and sister relationship" with a second or third spouse—hence, live as a celibate? With God's grace, all things are possible.

May an invalidly married couple who are willing to live as "brother and sister" receive holy Communion? With God's grace, all things are possible. Any such couple is urged to speak with a priest about the circumstances that could make such a relationship workable, and how, after receiving the sacrament of penance, they might well be able to manage it and to receive holy Communion, if they are prepared to sacrifice. As I mentioned at the outset, this book is not a "how-to" manual. It is, I hope, a guide to the possible and desirable.

I return to the "How dare you?" letter. To my knowledge, neither one of the divorced individuals whom I lunched with as a couple is Catholic. Both seem to me to be in good faith within the tenets of their own religious beliefs. My suspicion is that if they find in me or in some other priest an understanding, merciful representative of Christ, who tells them the truth, they will be either favorably disposed toward Catholicism, at which time their marital status could be explored, or they could become even more prayerful people than they seem to be right now, which is quite prayerful, indeed. In the latter case, I am confident that the good Lord will show them the path He wants them to follow. He can do that quite well without my advising Him–and certainly without my refusing to lunch with them.

Fidelity
in Marriage–
For Better
or for Worse

27

Cherishing Every Gift of God

This is not the first time I have written about Vickie. I have not seen her for more than thirty years, but she is as vibrant to me as my heartbeat. She was a little girl when I was in Monterey, brain-damaged, with an angelically beautiful face and black hair. Her picture is still on my wall.

On the first day of my First Holy Communion class for the retarded, Vickie sat still for perhaps one minute. Then, in her hard-heeled shoes she jumped up and stamped around the room creating chaos. To her utter shock, I put her out of the room and closed the door behind her until she knocked to come back in, but only to repeat the performance again and again and be ejected accordingly each time.

It took months, as I recall, for Vickie to settle down, a year before her mother, who attended every class, called to give me the thrill of my life. It was seven o'clock in the evening when the phone rang in my quarters. "Father O'Connor," Vickie's mother said in a voice running with tears, "you couldn't guess in a million years what happened this evening. As I have told you before, from infancy Vickie has never been able to eat with us at the table. She throws her plate into the air, dumps her food on the floor, screams at the top of her lungs. We have always had to have her sit on the floor in a corner by herself. Until tonight. For the first time in her life, Vickie ate at our dinner table with the family, serene, polite, a joy." Vickie's mother couldn't hold back her sobs any longer, nor could I. It was shortly thereafter that Vickie received her first holy Communion.

I write here of Vickie and her parents because they are far from being singular. Vickie could be born of any couple, rich or poor, of any color, race, or ethnic background, superlatively educated or completely unlettered. And although much has changed since I first fell in love with the Vickies of the world more than a half-century ago, I still find many parents shocked, confused, hurt, terrified by the birth of a retarded or "developmentally disabled" child. The same is true of parents who thought they had brought forth a "Gerber baby" at birth, only to be haunted as the years passed by the awareness that their child has Down syndrome, or is brain-damaged or otherwise radically different from what they had assumed.

It can be very, very hard. The temptation to have an abortion if amniocentesis or other testing predicts such a condition can be very great, and given our culture and its pressures, very understandable. Even greater can be the temptation to ask, "What did we do wrong? What sin did we commit? Why is God punishing me, or us?"

I will never forget stopping at a house on a parish visitation as a very young priest. In the course of the customary questions about Mass attendance, the sacraments, and related topics, I asked how many children the couple had. "Four," they told me. A deep sadness flooded me. I knew they had five. The fifth was in a bedroom upstairs, where they fed him, cleaned him, nursed him—and denied his existence. He was severely retarded. That's how guilty or ashamed some people can feel, and I understand that completely. Many don't know where to turn or what to do.

It's so unfortunate because they deprive both the child and

themselves, although without malice. Immensely demanding as the care of a child can be, for some parents a day and night affair, twenty-four hours a day, seven days a week, every week, every month, year after year. Yet what joy such a child can bring! Such a child can intensify and solidify the love between husband and wife and teach other children so much about the real meaning of family.

Yet fears run deep, and prejudices run even deeper. A cousin of mine took a little girl to a doctor many years ago, not sure whether she was simply a "slow learner" or retarded. The doctor took one look. "It's plain as can be she's retarded. That's what you get for having so many children." She was, in fact, a Down syndrome child, who grew up to be one of the happiest in her large family, radiating happiness to others. I buried her not long ago, when she was perhaps forty years of age, or a bit more. Never have I seen anyone mourned more deeply. She had become the living and beloved "glue" in the family.

I write of Vickie, however, not simply because she could be anyone's child, but because she's a symbol of the unexpected in marriage: unexpected sorrow, unexpected joy. She's a symbol, too, of the great potential of happiness to be found in the ordinary events of life that are so often meaningless to us because we take them for granted. "You'll never guess. Vickie ate supper with us tonight at the dining room table."

For better, or worse; for richer, for poorer; in sickness and in health, until death. Of the almost seven hundred Golden Anniversary couples who renewed their marriage vows in Saint Patrick's Cathedral on a Saturday after Easter, I wonder how many have had retarded or autistic or developmentally disabled children. How many have had perfectly healthy children who have disappointed them, abandoned them, abandoned their faith? In how many of these marriages that have perdured for so many years is one party afflicted with Alzheimer's, another with Parkinson's, yet another with cancer? How much unemployment have they known or financial insecurity? Has their been a lapse into infidelity, a drinking problem, a difficulty with in-laws? I have no idea; I know only how deeply I was touched by a husband pushing a wife in a wheelchair, a wife supporting a husband on a cane.

But what pride and joy I saw on their faces as they came to the altar rail to receive their certificates. They knew they had lived with and through the unexpected, they had walked at times in a valley of darkness, but for better, for worse; for richer, for poorer; in sickness and in health, they have lived their vows, they have given their love.

How fortunate the couple who find themselves cherishing every gift of God, however small. How fortunate a couple who are grateful for each other, for their health, for their children and the health of their children. How fortunate the couple who can be grateful, however difficult, for their sorrows, their disappointments, their seemingly insurmountable problems that so often are God's rainbows temporarily turned inside out, with joy ready to burst out of the clouds without warning. "Vickie ate with us tonight."

28

The *Real* Pastoral on Marriage

Go to bed, Dot," my father would urge my mother, comfortably dozing in an armchair. "Oh, Tom," she would plead, "I'm only resting my eyes. You go up. I have my prayers to say." My father, Tom, never needed any encouragement. Compared to him, Rip Van Winkle was an insomniac. He would shrug, check for the third time to see that the door was locked and the gas range turned off, and up he would go. A couple of hours later, with her neck bent out of shape, my mother would follow, but not until she had prayed a rosary and enough self-imposed other night prayers to make God ashamed of not releasing every soul from purgatory before dawn. Following this nightly prayerful marathon, my poor, wide-awake mother would go through the rest of the night, every hope of sleep gone with the final "Amen."

As I mentioned earlier, every year in Saint Patrick's Cathedral couples married fifty years or more renew their marriage vows, word by word, holding hands. Then I give each a certificate. Each certificate bears the names of the couple and, for a reason I am not certain of, my picture. I often think they should be giving me their picture, the picture in each case of heroic virtue personified.

Is *heroic virtue* too strong a term? Does it make accomplishing fifty years of marriage seem to be the equivalent of planting a flag on Iwo Jima in World War II, where "heroic valor was a common virtue"? Perhaps, but is anything less than extraordinary self-sacrifice required to make a marriage "work" for that long?

I cannot think of anything I have said in this book that would be so profitable to a young, engaged or married couple as would a visit to the brief ceremony of awarding these anniversary certificates. Couples come to the cathedral by the hundreds from the 185-mile length of the archdiocese. A husband in a wheelchair is pushed by a wife with a corsage. A wife is on a cane. Some look younger than springtime, some show the years. A wife tugs a husband's arm: "Come on, Harry. You're keeping the Cardinal waiting." I think of my father: "Come on, Dot. Go up to bed." And I am thinking, as well: *These couples have the right to keep me waiting all day.* A picture is snapped. The next couple is before me.

So many thoughts run through my heart as I shake a calloused hand, give a blessing, present a certificate. How have their children turned out? Have they brought this couple joy or suffering? Have there been many illnesses, or long, anxious nights of sleeplessness with a feverish baby, anxiety that a young daughter has not yet come home from a date, the shock of a stroke, the loss of a job? What has this couple endured in fifty years or more? What has brought them happiness beyond their dreams?

It's a wondrous thing to watch, and touch and feel the smile and the gratitude of these couples, a wondrous thing and humbling beyond measure. Every couple is a new, fresh version of O. Henry's story of the wife who cut off her glorious long hair tresses to sell, in order to buy her husband a gold chain for Christmas for his prized gold watch, while her husband was out selling his watch to buy her the hair combs he knew she longed for. That's the kind of love that comes up the aisle of the cathedral after fifty or more years of living a marriage.

Many of the anniversary couples are taken to dinner after the brief ceremony by children, grandchildren, others who are obviously as moved as I. The picture-taking goes on, I'm sure, until tired feet begin to ache and corsages wilt and reality recalls how far they may be from home and the chance to take their shoes off. They reminisce, they smile, they mostly listen. Some can't hear, some can't quite understand, some get a bit cranky after too many hours away from the daily familiarity of their own homes. But I have never heard a murmur of regret over renewing their marriage vows a half-century or more after they took them the first time.

What has really made the difference in their marriages? I don't have a shadow of a doubt. They are people of faith, a faith that perdures for better, for worse, for richer, for poorer, in sickness and in health—and will perdure until death. It's not a vague faith. It's very concrete. They believe in the Mass, in holy Communion, in confession, in the sanctity of even the least glamorous marriage, or in what seemed to be the most glamorous whose glamour has long since faded. Some are brilliantly educated, some can barely write. There are those whose English is limited. But they exchanged their vows a half-century ago and they will die with those vows intact.

I never see newspaper or television people at these simple ceremonies. There are no movie or TV "personalities" involved. They are largely out of *Saturday Evening Post* Americana, whatever their ethnic origins.

Anyone contemplating marriage, anyone already married, cannot help but be deeply influenced and inspired simply by watching these elderly anniversarians renew their vows of long, long ago. To them I say: Renew them and live them. They are the *real* Pastoral on Marriage.

Conclusion

29

The Abiding Sacramental Presence of Christ

I conclude these reflections on marriage acutely conscious that I have hardly scratched the surface of this profound mystery.

As a young priest more than a half-century ago I gave a Sunday homily on marriage that I'm sure was mercifully forgotten immediately after Mass by everyone present except myself. I used the words of a song old even then, but still known at the time by many. Forgive my repeating what I remember (all but one line). It was bad enough to use as a reminder of how little I knew.

"Two by two, they go marching through, those sweethearts on parade. Can't help sigh, as they pass me by, those sweethearts on parade. I'd love to join their army, but they bar me; for it takes more than one to join their army. Da da da, da da da da da (the only line I forget, but it was as silly as da, da, da, anyway), those sweethearts on parade."

Early in these pages, and intermittently throughout, I compared the sacrament of matrimony with the sacrament of holy orders. And whereas, of course, I had been given years of preparation for the priesthood by the time I was ordained, it has taken "a heap of livin'" as a priest even to scratch the surface of this mystery. The same is true, it seems to me, for any married couple, as it is for any priest. But one thing I suspect every couple learns quickly, as does every priest: Neither marriage nor priesthood can be lived as a passing parade, as if putting on a show for spectators. And every couple learns as well, I suspect, as does every priest, that—unromantic as it sounds—they alone are not enough for each other, any more than a priest is sufficient unto himself. We need, we desperately need, the abiding presence of Christ.

I am highly privileged in my living arrangements. Together with several of my brother priests and bishops I enjoy the great blessing of being able to reserve the Blessed Sacrament in a modest chapel in our house. Very early in the morning, late at night, any one of us can spend extended periods alone with the eucharistic Christ, in addition to our praying Morning Prayer together in the chapel each day.

Although some married couples are able to go to Mass each day, far more are virtually precluded by various obligations, and they don't have the luxury of the Blessed Sacrament in their homes. But as Jesus told His apostles before He ascended to heaven, "I will not leave you orphans." Married couples, it seems to me, can—indeed, must— seek Christ in each other and by way of His sacramental presence in their marriage. As we have noted before, He is there to turn water into wine for them spiritually as He did physically for the embarrassed young couple at the marriage feast at Cana. He is there to help them resolve their differences, quiet their anxieties, guide them through pregnancies and child care and illness and reversals of every kind. And far more than helping them handle problems, He is there to help their love become deeper and stronger as the years go on, to elevate it to a higher and higher plane, to give them a happiness far, far beyond even that exquisite wonder they may have believed on their wedding day would always be theirs.

I am blessed with a chapel, graced with the eucharistic Christ. How little I would "experience" that presence if I never visited Him, knelt before Him, thought about Him, listened to Him, conversed with Him in that chapel, feebly, told Him of my love, despite my sins, my stupidity, my awkwardness. A married couple are graced with the sacramental Christ. They administered the sacrament of marriage to each other, as each said, "I do." How much richer the marriage in which the couple together can turn to that Christ present sacramentally, visiting with Him, kneeling together before Him, telling Him their problems, their needs, their hopes and disappointments, their successes and failures, their foolishness and sins and love. In our little chapel we are all keenly aware that it is Mary who first made Jesus available to the world. It is my own conviction that in some way I don't begin to understand, He is continually with us "through" her in the Blessed Sacrament. Since it was she who intervened with Him on behalf of the married couple in need at Cana, surely the couple who turns to Him through her will have their needs met, as well. How a daily rosary can bind and enrich their love.

It's virtually a mystical relationship, I believe, that between marriage and priesthood. Fittingly do a couple exchange their vows before a priest and two witnesses, a priest whose own mother and father did the same. Fittingly do they offer the two elements of their own bodies to become a new entity, as the priest offers bread and wine to become the crucified and risen Christ. Fittingly must they sacrifice all, lay down their lives for each other and their children, as the priest must lay down his life for all of God's people. Fittingly do both married couples and priests find their fulfillment, their joy, and their peace in proclaiming to the world by the witness of their own lives the vibrant good news, the gospel of life itself.

This book leaves as much to be desired by its writer as for those of you kind enough to read it. Many, many chapters could be added, with the surface hardly scratched. As confessed at the outset, it is written by an unmarried man, but one who in all these years of priesthood has been privileged to help hundreds of couples prepare for marriage and counseled hundreds more whose marriages have been troubled, some to the point of desperation. To this admittedly limited degree I have written as an "insider," personal confidant to pains and sorrows and even heroic sacrifices, and as an adopted member of families blessed with great joy. No dimension of my vocation has been more personally fulfilling than that of helping couples prepare for marriage or working with them in their needs as the years have passed.

It is with gratitude burnished with awe, then, that I offer these simple thoughts and reflections to those preparing for marriage, as well as those who have lived this indispensable vocation for years. Perhaps in a small way it may supplement the help given by your own priest or counselor. Obviously, if one couple's marriage is enhanced a fractionfold by this little work, I will be deeply gratified. If not, it is reward enough for me to be given the opportunity to write of love, with love, to those in love or who want to recover a love that once was theirs.

Young lovers and old, you are in my every Mass and prayer. God loves you for your sacrifices. Thank you. Thank you so very much.